SELF-CHANGE

Strategies for Solving
Personal Problems

Also by Michael J. Mahoney

Behavioral Self-Control
Self-Control: Power to the Person
Cognition and Behavior Modification
Behavior Modification
Scientist as Subject
Permanent Weight Control
Abnormal Psychology

SELF-CHANGE

Strategies for Solving Personal Problems

Michael J. Mahoney

W·W·NORTON & COMPANY
NEW YORK

Library of Congress Cataloging in Publication Data
Mahoney, Michael J
Self change.
Bibliography: p.
1. Success. 2. Problem solving. I. Title.
BF637.S8M2155   158'.1   78-24243
ISBN 0-393-01176-3
1 2 3 4 5 6 7 8 9 0

To Mickey,
a very precious child

Contents

PART III: PERSONAL APPLICATIONS

Foreword

This is an attempt to translate some of the fundamental knowledge of modern behavioral science into specific and practical strategies for resolving everyday personal problems. It is not intended to be a substitute for psychotherapy, nor does it imply that self-change is something that can be achieved with very little effort. The main theme of the book is relatively simple: it is that *we are active participants in our individual dilemmas.* Problems are not just things that happen to us—they are complex experiences over which we have at least partial control. The principles and strategies discussed are therefore aimed at helping you maximize your control over personal problems.

The book is divided into three parts. In part I some basic principles are laid out. Chapter 1 talks about the pervasiveness of problems in everyone's life, and chapter 2 addresses the common myth that the only solution to personal distress is willpower. In contrast to some popular assumptions about heredity, modern theory and research suggest that human adjustment is primarily dependent on learnable *skills.* You are not destined to be depressed, obese, anxious, or otherwise dissatisfied with your life. These common problems are examined in chapter 3, which presents some basic information on the nature of personal problems. To say that a person "has" a problem is somewhat misleading since a problem is not a possession in the usual sense of that term. As outlined in chapter 3, a personal problem is basically an unsatisfactory feeling. More specifically, it is a feeling that things are not the way they should be. Their focus may range from your marriage to your bad habits, but the same general principles apply. Finally, chapter 4 outlines the fundamental strategies used by many professional counselors to identify and resolve a wide range of human dilemmas. These problem solving skills are relatively straightforward and do not require any unusual amount of intelligence or education for their successful application.

Having been introduced to the basic skeleton of personal problem solving in chapter 4, you will find part II of the book (chapters 5–11) devoted to a more detailed discussion and illustration of the skills necessary to address your own problems. Part III offers a guide to some of the most common causes and solutions of everyday problems and expands on some fundamental skills that may be helpful in individual applications. The final chapter (14) helps you to launch your own program of self-change.

There are, of course, hundreds of "self-improvement" books on the market. As I shall explain in chapter 1, this one is unusual in several respects. First, to my knowledge, the approach presented here is not offered in any other current book. This makes it unique, but, of course, may not say much about its value. For the average consumer of self-help books, it is difficult to evaluate the wild claims of effectiveness made by each and every author. A second unique characteristic of this book is that it does not contain such claims—it offers no extravagant promises of miraculous personality changes in less than thirty days. My personal and professional commitment is to helping, not selling, and the "system" outlined here is hardly a panacea for all human distress. It is, however, an accurate reflection of some of the most powerful and popular strategies employed by modern mental health specialists, and the promise of some of its methods has been amply demonstrated in dozens of scientific studies. These experiments and some of the theories which they have generated are cited in the bibliography at the end of the book.

Personal growth is not something that is achieved without effort, patience, or a minimum of discomfort. These may not seem like welcome or encouraging revelations in the foreword of a book on self-change. They are not meant to be discouraging, however. As a clinical psychologist, I am continually impressed with people's capacity to make very dramatic changes in their lives, sometimes after many years of relentless pain. My point is simply that self-change is seldom an easy or rapid achievement. It is, to be sure, richly gratifying, but it has its price: persistence, a willingness to try, and an openness to learning some basic skills. This is hardly the book for indivdiuals who are looking for an effortless personality overhaul— indeed, I would argue that such a book could never be honestly written. If you are willing to accept the fact that self-change will require some effort, time, and conscientious practice, however, you will, I hope, find this book both satisfying and personally relevant.

On a more personal level, I have many people to thank for their support and encouragement during the time I was writing this book. Besides the valuable assistance of Starling Lawrence and other Norton personnel, I am indebted to Sandy Ranio for helping me translate my piles of yellow notes into readable chapters. Thanks are also due to Diane Arnkoff, Kitty Mahoncy, and Guy Pilato. Being human, I have faced my own array of small and large personal dilemmas in the course of the writing, and these individuals' warmth and their willingness to support me in my own problem solving efforts have been much appreciated. They have helped me to learn much about myself and to understand that the satisfaction in traveling far exceeds that of arriving.

MICHAEL J. MAHONEY

I

Personal Problems
and
Their Resolution

1

Growing Pains

Maturity is the capacity to endure uncertainty.
—JOHN FINLEY

Benjamin Franklin has often been quoted as saying that two things in life are inevitable—death and taxes. Were he writing today, I would like to think that he would add a third item—personal problems. No matter how well you prepare or how cautiously you live, it is simply impossible to avoid painful or distressing experiences. I do not mean by this that life must be lived in perpetual dread or that it is an endless series of toils and troubles. It can be a richly rewarding experience in which our moments of occasional pain are more than offset by precious moments of joy and happiness. Nor do I take a dim view of the human capacity to cope. We humans are complex and versatile creatures—we have survived countless challenges and can be optimistic about surviving many more.

Yet if life is so joyous and humans are so versatile, why are personal problems inevitable? There are a number of possible reasons here, but I shall restrict myself to two of the most important. First of all, as human beings we are all born with the capacity to experience pain and unhappiness. Now this may not sound like an earthshaking observation, but it has important bearing on the question at hand. Have you ever wondered *why* we are capable of feeling pain and other unpleasant sensations? Are these the result of an accident by God or a freak mistake in evolution? Why can't we live our lives in bliss instead of struggling to overcome daily annoyances and unexpected tragedies? Strange as it may sound, *the ability to experience pain and distress is a very adaptive one.* Now don't jump to the conclusion that it is great to suffer or that people should try to *create* personal problems. Most of us are already good at the latter and need little encouragement. My point is that the world is organized in such a way that painful experiences are a necessary part of survival.

Imagine for a moment that you were asked to draw up some blueprints for a new animal—one which would be "better" and happier than humans. What capabilities would you give your bionic baby? Would you make it insensitive to pain—incapable of anxiety, depression, anger, and so on? After a moment's reflection you will probably be convinced that total insensitivity would be a mistake. Our capacity to experience pain is what helps us learn to avoid or escape dangerous situations. A child who was insensitive would be permanently handicapped in learning and very unlikely to survive. It is our sensitivity which helps us learn to avoid life-threatening challenges. Childhood burns, bumps, scratches, and bruises each contribute to our awareness (and respect) for an environment which can be threatening as well as fulfilling.

So what does all of this have to do with *your* personal problems? Remember that we are talking about the inevitability of pain and distress in our lives. One of the reasons for this inevitability is that we are "sensitive" creatures—that is, we have a nervous system which uses pain as a signal of danger and a cue for coping. Those of us who have survived our childhood have learned to avoid (or at least respect) sharp objects, deep water, heights, fire, and so on. In fact, we have learned to *anticipate* all sorts of dangers—to be on the lookout for threatening situations. This is useful when these situations are plentiful, but many of us have become oversensitive—that is, we may be overestimating the likelihood or intensity of a threat to our well-being. We must be sensitive to survive, but sensitivity has both assets and liabilities. It allows us to adapt—to learn survival patterns—and to experience moments of intense pleasure and satisfaction. On the other hand, our sensitivity allows us not only to experience distress but also to feel anticipatory pain. Our brain and nervous system help us to develop important associations (e.g., "fire danger") and to store these associations as memory. This is, of course, adaptive. But memory also makes us capable of reliving our past suffering over and over again, and our ability to anticipate dangers may become over-developed. We may exaggerate the dangers which lie ahead or may lose sight of the fact that they can be avoided or counter-balanced by future pleasures. These are just two of the patterns we will talk about in our later discussion of personal problems.

For the moment, our topic is inevitability. We have already discussed human sensitivity as one reason for the inevitability of personal distress. Another reason lies outside the person: namely, *our world is ever changing.* Adaptation is not a static undertaking in which you size up the world and then mold yourself to its demands. These demands will change with time, and the adapting person must be prepared to change with them. Think for a moment about the many stresses which are common to most us us *after* we have left high school, like—

moving out on our own
going to college or job training
serving in the military
getting married
moving
changing jobs
meeting financial obligations (e.g., buying a house)
having and raising children
incurring accidents and undergoing surgery

sustaining the loss of a close friend or loved one
suffering from recurring illnesses (colds, allergies, etc.)
sharing in the problems of our friends or children
going through the process of aging
losing a job
watching our children grow up and move away
retiring
experiencing terminal illness or death

These, of course, are only a few selected stress points in an average life. Our day-to-day existence is filled with many other stresses, large and small, which may alter over time. The point of all this, of course, is that *change is inevitable and often stressful.* Recent experiments by stress researchers suggest that even positive changes are stressful experiences. A job promotion, marriage, and a long-awaited baby may all be welcome changes, but coping with them often ushers in personal distress as new demands are made upon personal resources.

Life-Span Development

So far I have been arguing that personal problems are a common and inevitable experience partly because humans are sensitive to the demands of their world and partly because those demands are always changing. No matter what form it takes, change presents a challenge, and the adapting person is one who is relatively prepared to meet these challenges. Notice that I said "relatively": no one is ever absolutely prepared to meet any life crisis. Even the most skilled psychotherapist is subject to occasional distress, and I do not hesitate to note that I experience my own share of anxieties, anger, frustration, depression, and so on. This should not be surprising given that most psychotherapists are also human. While they may have developed some skills for personal problem solving, this does not mean that the personal problems never arise; it simply means that the skilled problem solver tends to experience more success in resolving the crises and predicaments which arise in all human lives.

I can remember a time in my own adolescence when I felt a sense of striving toward some vague future state called "maturity" in which my personal problems would melt away and my life would run smoothly. This is not an uncommon fantasy, and today's bookstores are filled with guides to guaranteed "togetherness," happiness, and all-round bliss. Many of these books seem to promise *arrival* at some elusive state of well-being which, once achieved, is never lost. Thus, millions of Americans are earnestly pursuing everything from meditation to megavitamins in hopes of getting their lives together and arriving at a state of private nirvana. While their efforts are understandable, their goals are—I think—sadly naive. Happiness is not a state which can be achieved and maintained. You are not likely to ever wake up and say "Ah-hah, here it is! I've arrived! From here on out, my life will run smoothly." As one popular maxim notes, *life is a journey, not a destination.*

None of us can achieve that elusive state of bliss that may have seemed just around the corner when we were in high school. Life will always present us with challenges and personal distress. This does not mean, however, that we are doomed to a life filled with unpredictable and unavoidable pain. While we may never "arrive" at some secure state of permanent tranquillity, we can at least prepare to cope with the challenges which may come along. It is my argument in this book that personal problems can often be dealt with in a direct and successful manner by means of a series of relatively straightforward techniques. Before we discuss these techniques, it might be worth examining how this approach compares with the hundreds of others which are currently on the market.

The Essence of This Book

There are now several hundred volumes on the market which could be loosely grouped into a category called "self-improvement." Some are specific in both their promises and their focus—they guarantee to make you more assertive, less obese, more sexually responsive, and so on. Others lean toward a more general promise of improved awareness, greater happiness, and better overall adjustment. Most contain dramatic case histories which illustrate how this or that strategy changed a person's entire life. The self-improvement strategies endorsed by these popular self-help books are equally diverse. They range from very specific exercises to rambling sermons on consciousness.

And yet here I am: writing yet another how-to-save-your-own-life recipe book—right? What possible grounds do I have for arguing that this book might be helpful where others are not? How can I possibly believe that this one is unique?

Well, to begin with, I am not arguing that every single self-help book now on the market is the worthless product of some charlatan. Many are well written and contain recommendations which are not unreasonable. The vast majority, unfortunately, cannot claim much scientific evidence in their behalf. This is rarely conceded by their authors, of course, who may be wildly enthusiastic about the miraculous powers of their pet therapy. But how are you, as a reader, supposed to know which techniques have been scientifically studied and which are the armchair conjectures of a self-proclaimed guru? Until we have some better controls over what is marketed as "psychotherapy," individuals in the general public will be at a loss to decide which approach is best suited to them. As it stands, you can't go by the title of the book, the credentials of the author, or even its claims to evidence. Virtually every self-improvement book has a catchy title, an M.D. or Ph.D. among its authors, and countless claims to prior success.

So how am I supposed to convey to you that this book is somehow different—and, I hope, better—than many which are already on the market? And more importantly, how are *you* to judge whether my confidence is well founded? In answering these two questions, I shall be previewing some of the themes and issues which will be emphasized in this volume. For purposes of clarity, let me list them.

First, unlike the vast majority of popular self-improvement book authors, *I will not promise to help you attain a permanent state of happiness.* Whatever else it may be, happiness is not something which can be captured and contained. It can, of course, be frequently experienced, and it is my hope that the strategies outlined in this book will help you experience more frequent and gratifying moments of happiness. You should bear in mind, however, that the underlying assumption here is that personal problems are inevitable. No one can totally escape them, but all of us can learn skills which will help us minimize their threat to our living a full and satisfying life.

A second point of departure between this book and some of its competitors is that, in it, I argue that *personal problem solving takes effort and skill.* This effort and skill are not beyond your reach, however, and you need not possess exceptional intelligence or willpower to develop them. In many of today's self-help guides, the secret to happiness is said to be "insight" or "awareness"—an intimate appreciation and acceptance of yourself and your world. While I am hardly an enemy of insight, I do not believe that awareness is usually sufficient to alleviate most personal problems. As I will explain in the next two chapters, awareness must usually be accompanied by action to produce a satisfactory resolution of a problem.

This means that there are no miraculous keys to nirvana, no overnight paths to inner peace. The resolution of today's—and your preparation for tomorrow's—problems will require effort, persistence, and a willingness to experiment. As you practice and refine your problem solving skills, of course, it will become easier to deal with the frustrations and pains which may lie around the next turn in the road.

A third difference between this book and others is the extent of its scientific backing. In contrast to the majority of today's self-help guides, *this book contains techniques that have survived considerable scientific research.* When I say "scientific research," I do not mean simply that there are files on numerous persons who have benefited from the techniques. Virtually every self-improvement author claims to have drawers bulging with glowing testimonials from past clients. Few of them report how many clients failed to improve, however, or how much improvement a person would have experienced without therapy. Case histories are a valuable means of *illustrating* how a technique can be applied, but they are not adequate in *demonstrating* that the technique is generally useful and apparently better than no treatment at all. These demonstrations can be accomplished only by rigorous scientific experiments in which trained investigators objectively assess the strengths and weaknesses of a technique.

If you will turn to the bibliography at the end of this book, you will find references to such experiments. The techniques presented in the following chapters are based on the results of these experiments—results which suggest that personal problem solving skills are a promising and helpful means to personal adjustment and growth.

Like life itself, however, science is an endeavor sprinkled with both success and failure, happiness and frustration. It would be a gross lie to say that *every* person who has ever tried to develop personal problem solving skills has been overwhelmingly successful. At this time, psychologists still have much to learn about how and why people act, think, and feel the way they do. We have made considerable progress in the last few years, but we are still a long way away from knowing it all.

Thus, the fourth and final difference between this book and

most of its competitors is that I admit that *I cannot absolutely guarantee you that the techniques in this book will be personally helpful to you.* I present them with a cautious optimism: they are the best we have at this time, but our best is unfortunately imperfect. You can be assured, however, that my confidence in their usefulness is shared by a large portion of my colleagues (see the bibliography). Indeed, I am essentially revealing some of the most respected professional strategies in the field. The techniques and steps outlined here are basically those used by many therapists in conducting psychotherapy and in working on their own personal problems. Hence, I am sharing with you what we believe to be our most effective techniques for coping with personal distress and promoting personal development.

This last point may have been somewhat disconcerting. If you are like most humans, you would like a written guarantee that this will work. Otherwise, why invest the time and effort? As much as I would like to be able to offer such a guarantee, my professional integrity and scientific conscience will not allow me to do so. All that I can say is, "I hope this will help —it is the best we have right now."

There are a few individual situations in which I would recommend immediate consultation of a qualified psychotherapist. These are basically situations in which there is a risk of imminent danger to yourself or someone else. If you are experiencing any of the following, I would recommend that you contact a therapist:

suicidal urges
a desire to harm someone else
frequent hearing of voices
blackouts or lapses of consciousness

Likewise, at the end of the book I will talk about the option of psychotherapy as a possible solution for your personal problems.

This volume is not intended to be a surefire substitute for professional counseling. I believe that it is, however, a worthwhile introduction to personal problem solving skills. As such, it may be sufficient for the dilemmas you are facing today and valuable in preparing you for the ones which are inevitable in your future. Let us now take a closer look at what those skills involve and how they may help you.

2

Willpower Versus Skillpower

What lies behind us and what lies before us are tiny matters compared to what lies within us.

— RALPH WALDO EMERSON

Pamela W. was a young nurse, happily married and in good health. She had been struggling for several years, however, with episodes of severe depression. When she was "blue," she would lie in bed all day. Pamela felt like she couldn't even muster the energy to pick up the telephone to inform her employer that she would not show up for work. This pattern gradually grew worse and had not been helped by two years of psychiatric counseling. When she came to see me, she told me I was her "last hope." She had begun to think that the remainder of her life was doomed to be full of sadness and passivity. Things looked hopeless to her, and Pamela felt that she was helpless in the situation.

One of the most common and pernicious elements in personal distress is the firm belief that "it can't be helped." This conviction is harbored by many people who seek counseling— and probably by many more who believe that even the counseling can't help. If you are like most humans, you know the feeling I am describing. Sometimes it may take the form of an intense dispair and a strong sense of helplessness. At other times it may feel like a nagging sense of self-doubt—a half-conscious awareness that one is fighting a losing battle and that defeat is inevitable. These feelings may vary from day to day, but they are usually most apparent in two situations:

1. When we are considering a plan of action which will require some effort (e.g., losing weight, quitting smoking, enrolling in school, and so on); and
2. When we are in the process of executing a plan of action (e.g., two weeks into our diet, halfway through a course, etc.).

Many people are aware that their self-doubts often become stronger when they are experiencing difficulty. It is much easier to be self-confident when the waters of life are calm than when they are stormy. Few people seem to realize, however, that their self-doubts can contribute to their difficulties. It is very hard to push ahead in some meaningful endeavor if one's head is filled with discouraging self-talk. Yet how many times have you caught yourself questioning your own abilities? "This will never work." "Who are you trying to fool: you know you just can't do this." These are examples of the subtle sabotage which we often tolerate in the privacy of our own thoughts. In many cases, the self-discouragement may be so much of a habit that we are not even aware of its occurrence.

There is now a growing consensus among professionals that many people "talk themselves into defeat" in their personal struggles. That is, they start off with a deep-seated pessimism and the expectancy that their struggle is a futile one. This expectancy can often operate as a *self-fulfilling prophecy* by helping to create the very failure it is predicting. In the case of Pamela W., for example, self-discouragement had become a vicious cycle. Pamela was convinced that she could not do anything about her depression. She lay in bed for hours every day crying over her helplessness. When she experienced an occasional glimmer of hope and an inclination to get up and do something, she quickly extinguished this flame by telling herself it was "no use." Pamela would then use her failure as proof of how futile things were. This started the cycle again, of course, and she began experiencing fewer and fewer moments of hope.

What am I driving at here? A couple of things—and they will be illustrated again several times before the book is through. First, it is common to have self-doubts in a difficult situation. Although you might prefer to go through life buoyed by unsinkable self-confidence, this is simply unlikely. When faced by a challenging situation, most of us become very self-conscious about our abilities. In one sense, of course, this is a reasonable and adaptive pattern. "He who hesitates is lost" may be an apt adage for a person who is trapped in procrastination, but "look before you leap" also has its merits. Unwarranted confidence may sometimes get us into considerable trouble, particularly when we have rushed into a difficult and important undertaking without first having gauged our competence.

For reasons I shall discuss in a moment, however, most humans need not fear being overconfident. This is not because most of us have good reason to feel inept but because our culture is one which tends to make us more skilled in self-criticism than self-confidence. From early in childhood we are taught that it is horrible to think well of ourselves—that it is "conceited" to pay ourselves a compliment (even when it is justified). After years of gentle brainwashing, many of us feel guilty about self-praise and compensate by going overboard in the other direction (that is, by being overly self-critical and apologetic). By the time we are adults, we are not only well trained self-critics, but we may also have come to *believe* that our negative self-evaluations are true. All too often, the "false modesty" encouraged in childhood may turn into unwarranted self-doubts in later life.

This is only one reason for our tendency to be critical of our performances and pessimistic about our abilities. There are many other common experiences which feed into this painful and paralyzing pattern. For example, ours is a culture which places great value on perfection. This was illustrated in the popularity of such books as *Jonathan Livingston Seagull,* the story of an ambitious character's attempts to reach perfection. "The Impossible Dream" may be an inspiring song, but it is also symptomatic of the broad theme of perfectionism that darkens so many lives. We strive to be best and to do something "perfectly—or not at all." The problem, of course, is that perfection is virtually impossible. Despite this fact, many people set goals for themselves which force them into formidable dilemmas. In our diets, our quit smoking programs, and sometimes even our relationships with other people, we get trapped in the saint versus sinner syndrome. Either we follow our diet religiously, OR we might as well binge. We are either a smoker OR a nonsmoker—there is nothing in between. Our marriage is either a success OR a failure.

Perfection is not only impossible: it may be counterproductive. As we strive toward being the ideal dieter, the total nonsmoker, and the perfect partner, we may develop two very dangerous tendencies:

1. the tendency to view our goals as all-or-none categories and
2. the tendency to look for and emphasize our failures over our success.

The all-or-none tendency is illustrated in our common practice of talking about our lives in an "on-off" fashion.

As if they were a light switch, we talk about going on or off a diet, being on or off the wagon, and being in or out of love. The unreasonable assumption, of course, is that there are no degrees between these two opposite extremes. One can be a partial smoker, a "sometimes" dieter, and a lukewarm lover without these necessarily being signs of failure. In fact, there is good reason to believe that the person who sets his or her sights on a more humanly possible goal will be more successful and satisfied than one who dreams the impossible dream. Our culture doesn't tolerate "wishy-washy" goals, however, and the person who takes aim at a nearer target may have to suffer occasional criticism for being a nonconformist.

Besides encouraging all-or-none views of life, perfectionism tends to make us overly sensitive to our mistakes. After all, when perfection is your goal, it takes only one error to put you out of contention. This is why so many people abandon their diets—and sometimes their marriages—after their first clear "failure." One forbidden sin, whether sweet or sultry, may convince them that they have "blown it." If they want a perfect life project (diet, marriage, relationship, job, etc.), they must scrap the old one and start another. Some go through most of their lives before they realize that that perfect project will never be enjoyed. The most satisfying lives are full of compromises, but many people don't learn this until late in the game.

A preoccupation with failure is hardly what the doctor ordered for the person who is deciding whether to begin some plan of action. If past failures seem to have been plentiful, it is easy to talk oneself out of even trying. Unfortunately, many people fail to realize that *there is a big difference between "I haven't" and "I can't."* The fact that I haven't been very successful in some important part of my life need not mean that I never will be. It might also mean that I simply haven't found the right solution. For many people, however, a history of personal failure may be viewed as evidence of personal inadequacy. This pessimistic outlook comes to influence their efforts and, eventually, their interest in attempting to change their lives. Note the vicious cycle here: a belief diminishes one's efforts, and the failure of these halfhearted efforts is then viewed as "proof" that the belief was correct. This pattern may be what Walt Kelly had in mind when he wrote, "We have met the enemy, and they are us."

At present, you may be convinced of your inability to change certain things in your life. Since you have read this far, however, I must assume that you have not totally given up—at least not yet. You may still be very skeptical, though, and you may feel that you have good reason to be pessimistic. After all, thirty dieting failures or a ten-year history of fearing airplanes may seem very compelling. There are, no doubt, some situations in which a problem can be resolved only partially, and we shall discuss these in more detail later. For the time being, I am concerned with your "readiness."

The approach outlined in this book does not demand blind faith or wild enthusiasm. But it does require your active participation and involvement. If you are convinced that it cannot help, it probably will not. This is not to say that your belief is its primary source of power. Rather, I am emphasizing that your beliefs may prevent you from giving it a chance—from exploring its promise for your individual circumstances.

Over the past ten years, psychological researchers have rejected a number of myths which had dominated the field for nearly a century. One of these is the notion that humans are "fixed" in their development once they reach adulthood. Earlier writers had argued that we developed firm personality patterns—often called "traits"—during our childhood and adolescence. By the time we were adults, our personalities were supposedly cast, and the cement had dried. Thus, through no fault of our own, we might be cursed with such traits as laziness, aggressiveness, or passivity. A second myth has to do with the concept of willpower. It had long been believed that persons who were successful in managing their lives were blessed with a mysterious thing called willpower. Those who had it were miraculously adept at self-control. They were organized and effective in their attempts to manage their lives. People who lacked willpower were doomed to being ineffectual.

These views have been dramatically challenged in the last decade, and many contemporary psychologists now emphasize the remarkable capacity for change which is evident in all humans—at all ages. We exhibit consistencies, of course, but they are not rigid. A depressed person need not be doomed to a life-style of depression, and the individual with a "temper" can learn to change this supposedly fixed aspect of "temperament." The concept of willpower has now been recognized as an explanatory fiction—that is, a concept which may appear to explain something, but which may actually be logically bankrupt.

When Jane loses twenty-five pounds, we may be tempted to attribute her feat to her possession of willpower. When Jack repeatedly fails to conquer his drinking problem, we may similarly attribute it to his lack of willpower. How do we *know* Jane has willpower and Jack does not? Well, she did lose twenty-five pounds, didn't she? And he has failed to stay off the bottle, hasn't he?

The problem here, of course, is that we have gone around in a circle. We have supposedly explained a behavior by invoking some mysterious inner force—but we have no evidence for that force other than the behavior it is supposed to explain! This is reminiscent of the mental patient who used to crack his knuckles to keep away elephants. When a psychologist pointed out that there were no elephants anywhere near the hospital, he said, "See there! It's working!"

More recent analyses of human behavior have given much more credit to *skillpower* than to willpower. It now appears that persons can learn to make dramatic changes in their lives, especially when they part with their old notions of being pushed and pulled by unrelenting traits. It now appears that old dogs can not only learn new tricks but that they can also become much happier in the process. Hundreds of experimental studies have now documented the remarkable versatility of humans when they are taught appropriate skills for managing their own lives. Even after many years of failure, an individual can learn effective methods of problem solving.

It is not my intent to "sell" you on some miraculous approach to self-betterment. As I mentioned in chapter 1, we are still a long way away from understanding all of the factors which influence human behavior. The strategies outlined in this book are, in my opinion, among the most effective and promising of those currently available. My concern in this chapter has been primarily to encourage you to explore their relevance for you, personally, and to alert you to the dangerous pattern of sabotaging your own efforts. While I cannot, with clear conscience, guarantee your success, I can assure you that these strategies have helped thousands of people to achieve more fulfilling lives. Many of those people had long histories of failure, and many began with more than mild skepticism. They did not, however, allow their skepticism to stand in the way of exploration. At this point, I shall therefore invite you to explore at least the next two chapters, which offer an overview of the perspective prescribed for problem solving.

3

The Nature of
Personal Problems

*Life is a mixture of unsolved problems, ambiguous victories and
vague defeats—with very few moments of clear peace. I never do
seem to quite get on top of it. My struggle with today is worthwhile,
but it is a struggle nonetheless and one I will never finish.*
                                                    —HUGH PRATHER

The everyday lives of John and Linda, who had been married
for six years, were dominated by bitter arguments. They just
couldn't seem to see eye to eye, and each was frustrated with
the other's shortcomings. John felt that Linda was careless
about finances and that she did not share in the responsibilities
of running their home. Linda thought that John was a compul-
sive and uptight spendthrift who was more interested in money
and a well-cleaned house than in her feelings. Their quarrels
were frequent and frantic, often ending up with John leaving
the house to get drunk and Linda crying on the phone to her
best friend. When they first came to see me, both were convinced that they were simply incompatible. They wanted a
professional opinion before they finalized their decision to file
for divorce.

Divorce can be a solution to marital problems, of course, and
yet many individuals mistakenly assume that divorce is a sign
of failure to resolve the problems in a relationship. In many
cases, separation or divorce may be the most reasonable and
satisfying option for both persons. Indeed, I have seen all too
many couples who have remained in a marital deadlock because

they feared the option of divorce. In these instances, preserving the marriage may have reflected a "failure" in the sense that it served no one's best interests.

But how does one know whether a particular course of action is for the best? Although it is not always easy, there are some general guidelines which seem to be helpful in making these decisions. While they may not offer absolute guarantees, they do at least provide one with the most confident assurance about important life choices. In this chapter we will examine the basic nature of personal problems. This will allow us the perspective required as we move on to a discussion of person problem solving in the next chapter.

What's the Problem?

Our first concern must be the nature of personal problems. What exactly *is* a problem? This may sound like a silly question since most of us feel that we have a good idea about the meaning of thic term. Indeed, we are familiar enough with our own problems to be able to recognize one when it develops. In the case of John and Linda, I asked each of them to state the problem in their own words. John's response was as follows:

> The problem is that she just doesn't care about money, or cleanliness, or keeping things organized. The house is a mess, our checking account is overdrawn, and I can never find anything because she never puts it away. That's the problem.

Linda, on the other hand, had a somewhat different view of things. When I asked her to describe the problem, she offered the following remarks:

> He is the problem. He is always complaining about money and housecleaning and . . . you name it. All he ever does is complain. A saint couldn't make him happy. That's the problem.

Which of them was "right"? Could both of their views be correct, or were they both off base? This depends, of course, on what one means by a problem. In the case of John and Linda, both had confused "the problem" with some of its possible causes. This can be a dangerous error in that it blurs the distinction between circumstances and feelings.

All personal problems are feelings. This does not mean that they are necessarily "in your head" or that there is nothing else to them. It does mean, however, that we tend to recognize a "problem" only when we recognize our *feelings* of dissatisfaction. But can't a person have a problem without knowing it?

We have all seen individuals who were careless with their money or who seemed to get drunk a little too often, and yet they may have been stubbornly reluctant to admit their dilemma. In many cases, this defensiveness is a sham; the person feels concerned about his or her conduct but is too proud or embarrassed to admit it. In still other cases, the person may not have felt any distress and—in at least this sense—they were not experiencing a personal problem.

For example, a woman recently consulted me about her husband's weight problem. He reluctantly accompanied her to a first counseling session, and I learned that he was not in the least concerned about his weight. In this instance, *she* was the one who felt dissatisfied, and the problem was more in the realm of her feelings than his. This does not mean that his obesity was not dangerous in terms of his health or appearance. We must recognize, however, that *a problem is always a felt discrepancy between the way things are and the way we would like them to be.*

This discrepancy may not be felt by everyone in the same way, nor are we all distressed by the same circumstances. Some of us are concerned about our personal adequacy or the meaning in life. Others are distressed about their relationships with people or their work. We each spend a sizable portion of our life worrying about the discrepancies we feel. On our way to work, in the solitude of our bath or shower, and in the quiet darkness of our bedroom, we are all consumed in a private struggle with our daily predicaments.

For some of us, that struggle gets no further than worrying —we spend the precious hours of our lives in anxious apprehension. Have we made a poor choice of marriage partners? Is *this* job the one that will really make us happy? Why do we feel a vague sense of threat in our future? Are we wasting our life in worry when we should be *doing* something?

In and of itself, worry is not our enemy. To be aware of our dissatisfactions—and to appreciate our dilemma—is perhaps the first step toward change. A person who does not feel unhappy is less likely to explore new possibilities in life.

On the other hand, worrying can become an impediment to our progress if we stop there. Like dreams, hopes, and all other forms of thought, worries can be a valuable call to action. They can act as signals for personal problem solving. The great danger with dreaming, thinking, and worrying is that they are easier to undertake than action. We can spend our lives lost in private fantasies which may be either pleasant or painful. Unfortunately, fantasies are costly substitutes for real life. As many of us learned during adolescence, the fantasies of our early years did not always prepare us for the reality of adulthood. Our storybook notions of love and life are often culprits in our later dilemmas.

I have tried to make several points here. First, a problem is always a felt discrepancy. Without the feeling, there is no subjective sense of a problem. A second emphasis has been that feeling distressed is an important first step toward personal change.

If you are currently struggling with depression, anxiety, or frustrations about your life, it may be hard to believe that these feelings are adaptive. The fact remains, however, that they are. Humans would probably have joined the dinosaurs as an extinct species had they not been capable of very painful feelings.

This does not mean that we should all strive to maximize our pain. Rather, it means that we should not lament the fact that we are capable of very unpleasant feelings. Our emotions are often our cues to take notice of our circumstances and to take action toward a more comfortable and adaptive movement in our lives. Such agonies as anxiety and depression are only maladaptive when we do not respond to them as important signals.

The final point in this section has focused on this very issue. It is easy to spend our lives lost in the privacy of our thoughts and worries. I will later argue that we can convert our thoughts from enemies into allies in our personal problem solving. For the time being, we need note only that our fantasies and private monologues may be critically important in our happiness and personal growth. We must take care, however, to insure that they do not become our tyrants instead of our tools.

What Causes Personal Problems?

I have just argued that "the problem" is never a situation or a person, but rather a feeling—specifically, a feeling of discrepancy. This means, of course, that the problem may be as individualized and different as are our feelings. It does not mean, however, that our life circumstances are irrelevant. Most of us do not feel distress in a vacuum: we feel distressed *by* something (e.g., our marriage, our job, our health, etc.). This brings us to a very important trio in personal problem solving —the *problem,* the *cause(s)* of the problem, and possible *solutions.* I have already noted that a problem is an unpleasant feeling of discrepancy between the way things are and the way we would like them to be. *The cause of a problem is always the cause of the discrepancy.* It is whatever it is that stands between present conditions and desired conditions.

It is very important to note here that *the cause of a problem is always current.* Many people tend to blame their current difficulties on things that happened to them a long time ago.

("I am unhappy because of my childhood." "I have never recovered from the death of my husband." "Phyllis had an affair two years ago, and I haven't been the same since.") If you closely examine statements like these, you will note how they try to place blame on something in the past. How is it possible for a *past* event to influence your *present* feelings?

It is possible only if that event left an impression which is still *current* in your thoughts. An unsuccessful romance, an unpleasant childhood, the death of a loved one—these are all very painful experiences. They continue to be painful, however, only as long as they remain a part of our current life. Am I therefore suggesting that we try to forget such things as quickly as possible? Not quite. It is often impossible to forget some of the most painful experiences of our lives. But as we shall see in a moment, we can prevent them from dominating our everyday feelings.

So far I have argued that the cause of a problem is the current cause of our felt discrepancy. But what is the cause of that discrepancy? At the risk of oversimplifying, it can be said that *the cause of a problem is always (a) a situation, (b) a behavior pattern, and/or (c) a thought pattern.* In many cases, it is a combination of these. Let's take, for example, the common problem of financial insecurity.

At one time or another, most of us have felt concern about money matters. What is the *problem?* It is our *feeling* that we don't have enough money to meet demands. In other words, there is a felt discrepancy between our present and desired income. What is the *cause* of this problem? It will vary, of course, from one individual to the next, but a common pattern is apparent. For many of us, the cause of our financial problem is—

1. that we may be receiving insufficient money (this is a situation); and

2. that we tend to spend more than we make *(a behavior pattern);* and

3. that we tend to worry about the discrepancy (this is a *thought pattern*).

Notice that we must therefore talk about more than one cause of our problem. This is a point to which we shall return.

Causes tend to be situations, behavior patterns, and thought patterns. Let's go back to the case of John and Linda. What was the cause of their marital dissatisfaction? As it turns out, there was not a single cause so much as a group of factors which contributed to John and Linda each feeling dissatisfied. John's distress, for example, seemed to stem in part from Linda's behavior and from his own expectations about how she should manage their home. That is, some of his standards were too high, and some of her behavior was unsatisfactory. To make matters more complicated, John was partly responsible for some of Linda's behavior. He was so critical of her that she was afraid to complete things for fear they would not meet his standards. Likewise, Linda's problem seemed to be a product of her unrealistic image of how a husband should behave and John's patterns of relentless criticism. Linda was also partly responsible for John's behavior since she created some very frustrating predicaments by never finishing things.

This example may sound a bit too complicated, but I chose it to illustrate several points about the causes of problems. First, note the former comment that *there is often more than one cause of a problem.* This is important to keep in mind when you are trying to figure out exactly what it is that is upsetting you. A second point which was illustrated was the fact that *we often contribute to our own problems.* That is, we frequently think or act in ways which aggravate our problems. The third—and perhaps most important—point to note here is that *all problems (that is, feelings of dissatisfaction) are caused by the way things are or the way we would like them to be (or both).* This is simply another way of saying that the cause of a problem is a discrepancy. It may be that the situation needs changing, but it is also possible that our goals merit reappraisal. Whenever we eliminate a discrepancy, we either change things to meet our standards, or we change our standards to fit our circumstances, or we compromise somewhere in between.

It is common for people to think that the cause of their problem is some factor in the external world. Thus, we find ourselves blaming the economy, our marriage, or our job for our personal dissatisfaction. It would be silly to deny that external circumstances can dramatically influence how we feel. On the other hand, we should recognize that our reactions to life events depend in part on how we view them. This point is illustrated in table 1 which shows how the same experience might produce very different reactions depending on how it was perceived. When person A receives her notice of termination, she perceives it as a tragedy which reflects on her worth as a person. It should not be surprising, then, that she feels depressed and apathetic. Person B also sees his termination in a negative light but interprets it as a sign of prejudice and persecution. It is thus understandable when he feels angry and resentful. Person C, on the other hand, perceives her termination as an unwelcome event but not a catastrophe or personal rejection. Her perception may be more balanced, in which case we would expect her to react in a more mature and adaptive fashion.

Now we all know that people react differently to the same situation. What am I saying that is different from that? First, we react differently partly because we may perceive things differently. Second, our reactions are partly influenced by our learned methods of coping with life's challenges—some of us have learned to cope more effectively than others. Finally— and this may be the most important point—the way we perceive things and how we cope with them can be changed. We are not a bundle of inflexible traits which push us toward high blood pressure, obesity, depression, and so on. Even though some changes may take time, we are all capable of improving

Table 1

	1. Situation	2. Perception	3. Assumption	4. Feelings	5. Action
Person A	Notice of Termination	"I've been fired."	Getting fired is a tragedy; it only happens to incompetent persons.	shame, depression, self-criticism	passivity
Person B	Notice of Termination	"I've been canned."	Those people are prejudiced; they've always been out to get me.	anger, resentment	retaliation (filing a grievance, vandalism, or bitter passivity)
Person C	Notice of Termination	"I've been laid off."	Getting laid off is unpleasant, but it happens to even the best of workers when times are hard.	disappointment	seeking an alternate job

our coping strategies. In the next chapter I will outline the approach which will be elaborated in part II. It is an approach developed by psychologists for helping individuals refine their patterns of personal problem solving. Before considering this approach, however, let us take a brief look at the nature of problem solutions.

So What's the Solution?

If the causes of a problem are situations, behavior patterns, and thought patterns, it should not be surprising that *effective solutions to a problem are those which change the appropriate situation, behavior pattern, or thought pattern.* To change how we feel, we must change the discrepancy between the way things are and the way we would like them to be. How? By making changes in those areas of our life which are contributing to the discrepancy. How might we alter the situation? To what extent would a change in our behavior lead to a smaller discrepancy? Are we perceiving the circumstances accurately? Are our goals realistic to our means? These are obviously important questions, and their answers may reveal very welcome solutions to our personal problems.

It is important to note that a correct identification of the causes of a problem may be one of the most crucial steps in determining the right solution. In the case of John and Linda, it was decided that a mutual change was indicated. John agreed to watch his critical remarks and to try to lower his standards regarding Linda's behavior. In return, Linda agreed to organize her work in a way which would make it easier to complete. Since they had developed a pattern of daily bickering and arguing, they also decided to have a nightly session of less aggressive exchange. Every evening, just before the late show, they spent ten minutes expressing appreciation for one another's efforts and offering kind feedback on their mutual progress.

Not all marital bickering can be successfully altered by such a simple strategy. One of the underlying assumptions of this book is that *all personal problems are unique.* Only you have exactly your genetic makeup, your learning history, your memories, and so on. Thus, each problem must be approached on an individual basis. On the other hand, we now have some idea about general principles of problem solving which can be applied to these individual instances. In the next chapter I shall outline those principles, and we shall then move on to their application in your life.

Since this chapter may have offered some new ways of looking at personal problems, it might be worthwhile to summarize its main points. First, recall that there is an important difference between (a) a problem, (b) its cause, and (c) its solution. A problem is always a feeling. More specifically, it is a felt discrepancy between the ways things are and the way we would like them to be. The cause of the problem is always the cause of that discrepancy, and it is always current. We talked about the fact that many problems have more than one cause and that these causes tend to be (a) situations, (b) behavior patterns, and/or (c) thought patterns. The way we act and our pattern of thought often contribute to our predicament. Fortunately, we humans are flexible creatures, and we can learn to change our patterns of experience. Thus, when we arrive at a solution to our problem, it is always a strategy for changing our situation, our behavior, or our thought patterns. These changes may require large or small adjustments in our life-style, depending on the nature of our problem.

What is important to remember is that you can always do something to reduce your distress. If you think things are hopeless or that you are incapable of change, then it is these *thoughts* which deserve your earliest attention in a personal problem solving (PPS) project. Now let's see what such a project might look like.

4

Personal Problem Solving (PPS)

The whole of science is nothing more than a refinement of everyday thinking.

—EINSTEIN

Have you ever wondered why some people seem to have more problems than others? Each of us probably knows someone whose life seems to be an endless series of struggles—a person who moves from one crisis to the next and often comes out on the short end of predicaments. You may, in fact, think that this description applies to you—particularly if your personal problems seem to be frequent and unending. Why is it that some people seem to glide through life in relative calm, with only occasional dilemmas and rare tragedies? Is it an accident or an example of divine inequity?

There is little doubt that we are each a victim of different circumstances and that these circumstances can have a dramatic influence on the richness of our life and the nature of our personal problems. But there is more to it than being a passive victim of circumstances. As noted in chapter 3, we each must take responsibility for some of the circumstances of our life. True, you cannot help being as tall (or short) as you are, and it is impossible to undo the effects of a paralyzing auto accident. You can, however, handle daily challenges and your overall life situation in ways which will make you happier and more satisfied.

This last point is illustrated time and again by individuals who seem to be at great disadvantage but who "succeed" despite their circumstances. John R., for example, was a twenty-four-year-old veteran of the Vietnam war. He was married and had two children when he was sent overseas. During an enemy attack, John was hit by shrapnel from an exploding grenade: his face was permanently disfigured, and he was blinded. His initial reaction was understandable—severe depression, anger, and embarrassment. He would never again *see* his children, and he knew that his face was now pitted with scars. How could he expect his wife to love him? Or his children to want to see him? John, however, was a good problem solver, and his brief period of dejection was followed by some active planning. He assessed the situation, taking an objective appraisal of the real damange and closely examining the options which lay before him. Within a few months, he was learning to read braille and had applied for veterans' benefits to help him pursue an education in counseling. Not surprisingly, he was interested in helping others who were struggling with the agony of a physical handicap.

Terry S., on the other hand, had never had any physical handicaps. She had grown up an only child in a well-to-do family, and she had never been deprived of anything. Her childhood read like a Shirley Temple movie—full of toys, servants, and mountains of ice cream. When Terry went away to college, however, she began to show signs of emotional distress. She began to gain weight and complained of insomnia. With her parents' money, she was able to see some of the top medical specialists in the country, none of whom could find any medical disorders. Gradually, Terry began to get worse. She missed classes and gained over sixty pounds. When she finally flunked out of school, she was referred for psychological counseling.

What is the difference between people like John R. and

Terry S.? The one seems to succeed despite formidable obstacles while the other has every worldly advantage and yet develops serious psychological problems? Many people would try to explain their difference on the basis of willpower or some other mysterious inborn strength. As we saw in chapter 2, however, willpower is not a very useful concept when it comes to explaining human adjustment. Many psychologists would now argue that a large part of the difference between John and Terry is their personal problem solving *skills*. Somewhere along the line, John had developed skills appropriate to meeting the challenge presented by his physical handicap. Terry, on the other hand, had led a pampered life in which all important decisions had been made for her. She had not had the opportunity to develop some of the skills which are necessary in order to cope with daily demands. This deficit became obvious when she was forced to leave home and enter a strange situation (college) which demanded independent living skills.

Now this is obviously an after-the-fact interpretation. Can we be *sure* that the main difference between John and Terry was their problem solving skills? No, we cannot. However, there is now a sizable body of research which is consistent with such an interpretation. Studies cited in the bibliography of this book have closely examined the personal problem solving skills of persons experiencing psychological problems and those who seem to be better adjusted. The results of these studies are clear: persons with recurrent emotional problems tend to be inferior in their problem solving abilities. More impressive, perhaps, are another group of studies which suggest that these same people can *learn* personal problem solving skills and that training in these skills often leads to significant improvements in their personal happiness and overall adjustment.

Such research is, of course, the rationale for the present book, and part II will be exclusively devoted to the problem solving skills which seem to be important for personal improvement. Before we look at the specifics, however, it might be worthwhile to take a brief glance at the big picture. What exactly are these skills?

Personal Science

To many people, a scientist is a person who spends his or her life locked away in a sterile laboratory. It is therefore not surprising when people raise their eyebrows at the thought that *a person who is good at resolving personal problems is, in effect, a good "personal scientist."* Whatever else they may be, scientists are professional problem solvers. They are trained to recognize problems, to identify their causes, and—in applied fields —to develop effective solutions. The person who is skilled at solving personal problems is in many regards no different from the scientist. That is, the skills which are required in good scientific research are essentially the same skills that are helpful in adaptation and personal growth. Does this mean that you have to have a degree in chemistry or a microscope to solve your problems? Hardly. The specific skill requirements are different depending on whether you are working on a problem in nuclear physics or on a conflict in a love relationship, but the general skills are very similar. Let me illustrate.

Let's take a common everyday problem involving an automobile. All of us have probably experienced frustration over a car which stalls or misfires. Note that the problem is our *feeling* of frustration over the discrepancy between the way our car behaves and the way we would like it to behave. Assuming you are not one of those people who immediately takes the car to a mechanic, what are the steps you go through in solving an automotive problem? Well, to begin with, you probably try to determine exactly what the problem is. Is it lack of power, dying at traffic lights, idling very roughly, or what? Next, you probably begin to turn into a "super sleuth"—looking for clues to the mechanical crime. You begin to collect information so that you can come up with ideas about the probable causes of the problem. Recall from chapter 3 that we talked about three different categories of causes: situations, behavior patterns, and thought patterns. Is there something wrong with the car itself? Could it be something you are doing (a behavior pattern), such as the way you drive it or the type of gas you are feeding it? What about the possibility that the car is fine and that your frustration stems from unreasonably high standards for a 1955 Studebaker?

Let's say that you have decided that the problem does not stem from your standards (thought patterns). It is still possible that there is something wrong with the car itself or that you are behaving in a way which causes it to act strangely. To check out the latter, you may switch your brand of gasoline and experiment with the speed at which you accelerate and with other aspects of your driving. Assuming that the car's misbehavior does not clear up, you are left with the probable conclusion that there is something wrong with the car itself. It is here that some of us may take different paths in our problem solving. If we are amateur mechanics, we may run through an imaginary list of possible causes (and, hence, possible solutions). Could it be the spark plugs? The air cleaner? The timing? The mechanically brave will venture forth out into the garage and experiment with solutions to one or more of these problems. Those who are less skilled mechanically will talk to a friend or take the car to a service garage. There, the mechanic will probably ask to be filled in on the earlier stages of problem solving. What is the problem? When did it start? When does it get worse or better? What solutions have you tried already? If the mechanic's solution is successful, our feelings of frustration are reduced, and we go back to life as usual. If the solution is a failure or only partly successful, however, we will persist in our problem solving, demanding a "better" solution from the mechanic or, in extreme cases, selling the car and buying a different one.

It may not have been obvious, but the problem solving

which took place in the above example followed a series of stages which are common to almost all instances of problem solving. These seven stages make up the basic strategy of scientific inquiry, and they can be represented by the seven letters in the word "science":

S   Specify the general problem area.
C   Collect information.
I   Identify possible causes.
E   Examine possible solutions.
N   Narrow solutions and experiment.
C   Compare your progress.
E   Extend, revise, or replace your solution.

In the first stage of personal problem solving, one tries to define the problem. What exactly is making you feel badly? In the foregoing example, it was the discrepancy between ideal car performance and that being observed in the Studebaker. This stage is usually followed by a phase of information gathering. (How great is the discrepancy? How often does the car perform poorly? Does it perform better—or worse—in cold weather? When the gas tank is almost empty? When the engine is warm?) Collecting such information usually leads to ideas about possible causes, and causes, of course, often suggest solutions. If the cause is a dirty carburetor, for example, one can consider such options as (a) buying a new or rebuilt carburetor, (b) adding a can of carburetor cleaner to one's next tank of gas, (c) asking a mechanic to clean the carburetor, and so on. Before experimenting with one of these possible solutions, one tentatively eliminates the others—that is, narrows the field to one's "best bet" and tries it.

The outcome of this experiment is then evaluated. How does the car's current performance compare with its performance prior to the experiment? Is it better? Worse? About the same? This comparison, of course, leads to still another decision. If the solution was completely successful, then you will probably continue (extend) it. If it was only partly successful, you may want to revise the solution by adding another option. Finally, if it was a failure, you must retrace your steps and replace the unsuccessful solution with another option.

Now what does all of this have to do with *your* current problem? If you are trying to lose weight, conquer insomnia, control your spending, or overcome your feelings of insecurity, the example of a misfiring car may seem far afield. I chose this example for its simplicity and frequency, not because it is the best or the only illustration of a personal problem solving approach. But the personal science sequence outlined above can be applied to a wide variety of problems, and its flexibility is almost infinite. That is, regardless of the personal problems which you are now facing, there is a very good chance that the personal problem solving (PPS) sequence will help you clarify the problem, identify possible causes, and experiment with effective solutions.

Since each of the seven stages requires some specific skills, a separate chapter will be devoted to each in part II. Before we move on to those skills, though, it might be worth offering a second illustration of the possible promise of this approach for your life.

Stephen L. was a successful businessman who had worked his way up through the ranks of a large corporation. He had a fine home, a happy family, and was well respected in the community. As his success continued over the years, however, he began to feel increasing pressure to excel. Last year's accomplishments had to be surpassed by this year's promotions. To do "well" was taken for granted; he felt that he had to make each year a new pinnacle of achievement. He began spending extra hours at the office, and his interactions with his family started to deteriorate. His blood pressure went up, his promotion fell through, and Stephen was soon finding himself a frequent customer at local taverns. What had started out as an occasional martini at lunch had now escalated to nothing but alcohol at noontime and a ritualistic stop at a bar before he went home. One night he had consumed a bit more than usual, and while he was driving home, he narrowly missed hitting a child. He called for counseling the next day.

In terms of the personal problem solving (PPS) sequence, Stephen was first asked to clearly define his problem. This was not difficult since he was feeling great concern over his accelerating pattern of drinking. He was then asked to move on to the second stage of PPS (that is, to collect information). Stephen was given a diary in which he was asked to write down, over the next week, the circumstances surrounding his drinking. When did it occur? Where? What thoughts or feelings preceded it? Was he alone or with a friend? This information was useful in identifying possible causes of the drinking (stage three of PPS). Remember that causes are factors which contribute to the felt discrepancy between the way things are and the way one would like them to be. Was it Stephen's work situation? Aside from the drinking itself, did some of Stephen's behaviors contribute to the problem? What role did his thoughts play? After over a week of sleuthing, it was clear that at least one thing was consistently associated with Stephen's drinking: thoughts about work pressure and failure. According to his diary, he often thought about the demands of his job and the problems he was having at home—and these thoughts were particularly apparent around lunchtime and on his way home. He was afraid he would fail to continue his successful business record and that his family would be disappointed in him. When his last promotion fell through, this simply added fuel to the fire. He was now obsessed with daily thoughts of impending disaster and family embarrassment.

But what to do? What were his options? Recall from chapter 3 that problem solutions always involve changes in a situation, behavior patterns, or thought patterns. Stephen looked closely at his work and home situations: neither seemed in need of change to help him with his drinking. Although he felt dissatisfied with the way things were going at work and with his family, he saw this as being the *result* of his drinking rather than the *cause* of it. The main behavior he wanted to change, of course, was his consumption of alcohol. In the third category —thought patterns—Stephen found a host of things that seemed like likely candidates for change. His obsessive worrying and his inflationary standard setting seemed to be frequent culprits in his drinking. He decided that these thought patterns needed some serious alteration. But how?

With some technical advice from his counselor, Stephen made out a list of possible solutions (stage four in pps). It included the following:

1. Join Alcoholics Anonymous.
2. Simply tell myself to think differently.
3. Take a continuing education course on meditation and self-confidence.
4. Pursue psychotherapy for obsessive worrying and perfectionism.
5. Develop some homework assignments for reducing worrying.

After some deliberation, Stephen decided to eliminate the first, second, and fourth alternatives. They were not ruled out permanently, but he simply felt that they were less promising solutions at the time. This left the field narrowed to two remaining options, and he decided to combine these and experiment (stage five in pps).

Stephen enrolled in a six-week course on transcendental meditation—a course which was designed to help him relax and to teach him methods of controlling various patterns of thought. At the same time, he purchased a book recommended by his counselor for its relevance to problems of perfectionism and worrying. The book helped him develop homework assignments in which he identified and evaluated some of his long-held beliefs about work performance. In one assignment, for example, he asked himself to write a criticism of the philosophy that "to feel good about yourself, you must always do better than you have done in the past." Assignments like this one seemed to help him challenge his perfectionistic standards, and the meditation training made it easier to "turn off" many of his daily worries about failure. Thus, when he looked at his progress two months later (stage six in PPS), he was quite pleased.

Stephen was still experiencing occasional periods of extreme worry and work anxiety, but his diary suggested that they had decreased in both frequency and intensity. Likewise, although he had become moderately drunk twice during the two-month period, this was dramatic improvement over his earlier pattern. It was, in fact, reassuring that he was not perfectionistic in evaluating his progress (demanding that either the problem be solved or that he consider himself a failure). Stephen recognized the progress he had made and decided to continue the solutions he had selected (stage seven in PPS). His family was very supportive of his efforts, and—somewhat to his surprise—he received a promotion the next year despite the fact that he had relaxed some of his standards.

To fully appreciate the stages in Stephen's problem solving, of course, one would require a more complete understanding of some of the skills entailed in each of the seven phases of PPS. However, I hope this illustration has pointed out that the personal scientist sequence has very clear relevance for difficult personal problems. Clinical scientists have now reported successful applications of similar strategies to such problems as anxiety, temper tantrums, marital problems, obesity, delinquency, and a wide range of other patterns. Examples of some of these applications will be given as we investigate specific skills in part II.

II

Principles of
Personal
Problem Solving

5

Specifying the General Problem

To be human is not a fact, but a task.

—KIERKEGAARD

In the first stage of PPS, your primary focus is on defining the problem. In one sense, of course, all problems boil down to the fact that "I feel differently than I would like to feel." Feelings do not exist in a vacuum, however, and stage one requires that you try to link these feelings to various realms in your life. In a sense, you are trying to identify the challenge which confronts you. What is it that I am struggling with?

In some cases, this may seem very obvious. If you are trying to lose weight, for example, you are likely to jump to the assumption that your problem is already specified: you are overweight. Recall from chapter 3, however, that a problem is always a feeling. It may be that you are *feeling* depressed or anxious about your weight, and this would constitute a more accurate specification of the problem. In other instances, identifying the problem may be somewhat more complicated. Consider, for example, those moments we have all experienced when we knew that something was vaguely wrong, but we just couldn't put our finger on it. How do we go about specifying a personal problem when it seems vague or complicated?

Whether vague or clearcut, complicated or simple, a personal problem can usually be specified by examining two basic questions:

1. How do I feel?
2. Where do I feel this way?

The first question may seem like a simple one to answer, but many of us are poor at describing our feelings. For some people, of course, feelings are easy to identify. "I feel anxious . . . hurt . . . frustrated . . . depressed . . . helpless." In stage one of PPS, it is often a good idea to sit down and simply look at your feelings. This is most readily accomplished when you are alone and without distractions. What is it that you are feeling? Can you compare it to a feeling you have had in the past? Do you feel nervous, jittery, or apprehensive? Or is it more like anger and hostility? Do you feel like crying, running away, or fighting? Questions like these can help you identify some of your feelings and this, in turn, will take you a step closer to specifying what you would like to feel after some personal problem solving.

Let me illustrate this important first element in defining a personal problem. Dorothy H. was a friend who had asked me to go out to lunch. As we were sitting in the restaurant, I noticed that she seemed unusually quiet. When I asked her if she was all right, she said, "Yes, but I've been out of sorts for the last few days." I asked if she could elaborate on what it meant to be "out of sorts," and she said, "Well, that is part of the problem. I know I'm feeling badly, but I just can't seem to put my finger on it or to figure out why."

Jumping to the cause of a feeling before you have identified that feeling can sometimes get you in trouble, so I pursued my questioning about *what* she was feeling before moving on to *why* she was feeling that way. I asked her if she could describe her sensations at all. She closed her eyes and said, "Well, it's like swirling around and the whole world seems to be at a distance—almost like I have backed up from it or something."

I asked her if she could compare it to any feelings she had ever had before. She thought for several seconds and then remarked, "I remember once in grade school feeling something like this. I was sort of lonely. . . ." I asked her what had happened before that experience in grade school. "Well, I think it was right after I lost a class election. I had been running for vice-president, and it seemed so important at the time. When I lost, I just felt like withdrawing from everything and being by myself."

As we talked, it became clearer that Dorothy was experiencing some feelings of depression and loneliness. We were later able to relate these feelings to a recent setback she had experienced in a close relationship.

Knowing *how* you feel is only part of the question, however. It is also important to be able to specify *where* you feel that way. By this I don't mean in what part of your body, but rather in what part of your life. Are your feelings coming from a specific area? Your work? Your finances? Your relationship or marriage? Your health? If you can identify a specific realm of discrepancy, you may be better prepared to examine possible causes and solutions. In some cases, of course, this will be impossible.

For example, if your feelings of depression or anxiety stem from a global sense of personal inadequacy, it may seem like all realms of your life are affected. You may lack confidence in your work, your relationships, your financial security, and so on. This does not necessarily mean that a PPS strategy is inappropriate, but it suggests that your search for causes and solutions will have to be broadly conceived. Knowing whether your feelings of dissatisfaction stem from a restricted area of your life or whether they pervade all realms can therefore be helpful in suggesting ways in which you may want to approach their alteration.

When you have arrived at a tentative specification of a

general problem, you may already be close to setting some goals. To say that your unsatisfactory feelings seem to be related to your health is to say that you want to either lower your standards or improve your health. At this stage, it is important to repeat a comment made earlier about goal setting. Goals can be very helpful in personal problem solving projects, but they can also lead to disaster when they are unreasonable. If you set perfectionistic goals which are nearly impossible to achieve, you should not be surprised if your PPS project fails to attain them. Thus, it is often helpful to separate your goals into two parts: *short-term goals* which you hope to achieve during the next few days or weeks, and *long-term goals* which are more remote targets for achievement. In both cases, of course, it is important to be realistic. If you are fifty-four years old, it would be silly to set a physical fitness goal that is more appropriate for a teenager.

Long-term goals are those elusive ideals way off in the distance. They may stay in the back of your mind as an incentive to continue in your PPS pursuits. Much more important, however, are the short-term goals, for they help to motivate and direct your daily efforts toward self-change. The relative importance of these two types of goals was recently illustrated in an experiment conducted by Albert Bandura and Karen Simon of Stanford University.

Overweight persons were asked to count the number of bites they took and were divided into two goal-setting groups. In one group, participants were asked to set daily goals for reducing their eating behavior (that is, taking fewer bites). Persons in the other group set weekly goals. After only one month it was already clear that persons who set short-term (daily) goals were achieving much more success than persons who set more distant (weekly) goals. Weight loss in the first group averaged 6.5 pounds as compared with almost no change in the second group. When we discuss the skills involved in selecting and experimenting with solutions to personal problems, we will return to this important issue of goal setting.

It is not uncommon for people to be experiencing more than one problem. I can remember times in my own life, for example, when I have been depressed in one realm, anxious in another, and frustrated in a third. What should one do in these predicaments? There is no simple answer to this question although some general comments may be helpful. First, ask yourself how urgent your problems are. If you are seriously considering suicide or if you are panic-stricken over something you have to do in the next day or two, this may not be the best time to refine your problem solving skills. These are situations which require more immediate attention, and your best alternative may be to consult a qualified professional. The skills involved in personal problem solving are not excessively difficult, but they do take some time and practice to master. It is therefore more appropriate to embark on PPS training when you are facing problems which do not involve imminent or urgent consequences.

Suppose your problems are neither a matter of life or death nor something that *must* be dealt with in the next few days. What then? How do you decide which of your problems to tackle? Should you attack all of them at once or work on them one at a time? The answer here seems to be fairly clearcut: *it is almost always better to work on one problem at a time.* People who try to overhaul their lives in one grand program of self-change are seldom as successful as those who patiently work on one realm of functioning and then gradually move on to another. If you would like to quit smoking, lose weight, develop an exercise routine, and overcome your fear of flying, you are better off to tackle one of these and move on to another only when the first is in a state of acceptable progress or resolution.

This point raises the obvious question: which problem should I tackle? Here, the scientific literature is less certain, but it would appear that *you are better off to begin with your least difficult problem.* The idea, of course, is to have you start with something more likely to be an early success so that you will develop some of the basic PPS skills and gain some confidence in your ability to produce meaningful changes in your life. If you have successfully developed a program of exercise and maintained it for several months, you may be more optimistic and motivated when you undertake your next PPS project.

How do you know ahead of time which problems are less difficult? There are some situations in which this may be hard to decide, but some general remarks may again be helpful. For the most part, a personal change is easier—

1. when it involves a relatively small and comfortable alteration of daily habits (e.g., switching to decaffeinated coffee);
2. when it emphasizes *doing something* instead of *not doing something* (e.g., jogging instead of not smoking);
3. when it has the support and encouragement of important friends and family members;
4. when it is undertaken with very modest goals which are very gradually increased over time;
5. when there is immediate and important payoff for making the change;
6. when the pattern being changed is recent in development.

Although it is difficult to generalize across individual situations, it is safe to say that smoking as well as alcohol and drug abuse are some of the more difficult personal problems to change. Thousands of individuals are successful every year, but countless others fail in their efforts. Thus, if you would like to work on one of these problems and there are others which also need your attention, you may want to postpone the more difficult ones until you have developed and polished some of your PPS skills. If you do not have another problem which you could use for "practice," you should of course proceed, and you need not be pessimistic about the outcome. The three problems mentioned above are more difficult, but they are hardly unconquerable. With some patience and practice, your chances for improvement or resolution are very good.

One final point should be made before we leave the topic of which problem to work on. As mentioned above, it is generally better to work on that problem which is most easily remedied. You should not, however, choose a problem which you are not motivated to solve. Do not, for example, decide to develop an exercise program simply because it is supposed to be easier than quitting smoking. If you are not sincerely interested in becoming more physically active, you will not invest sufficient energy in your PPS project, and the chances are good that you will quit before you have attained a satisfying change. The point here is that your PPS project must be important to you. Don't choose an easy one which is personally uninteresting. It is better to tackle a difficult personal problem which is very important to you than to conjure up an easier one just for the sake of practice. With this point in mind, let's move on to stage two of PPS—collecting information.

6

Collecting Information

There is a price to be paid for every increase in consciousness. We cannot be more sensitive to pleasure without being more sensitive to pain.

—ALAN WATTS

If you are old enough to remember Jack Webb in the television series "Dragnet," you will perhaps recall his most famous line when he was investigating a crime: "All we want are the facts, ma'm, just the facts." In PPS, *personal "facts" play a very important role in successful self-change.* Many people who attempt to change some aspect of their life go about it in a rather haphazard fashion. They suddenly decide that they need to improve their sleeping patterns or reduce their spending, and they jump into a self-change project without any clear understanding of some of the factors which may be contributing to their current problem.

A case in point was a middle-aged housewife, Sue W., who had decided that she needed to lose forty pounds. We had met at a party, and when she heard that I was a specialist in self-control, she began to describe the rather Spartan diet she had adhered to for over ten days. Advertised in one of the popular women's magazines, it required that the dieter live on about five hundred calories of protein and nothing else (except some vitamin supplements). Sue was already feeling some of the side effects of the diet and had lost less than half a pound.

I asked her how many calories she had consumed per day *before* she started the diet. She said she didn't know. She was very surprised when I commented that a sizable percentage of overweight women are *not* overeaters—that is, they do not consume an excessive amount of calories. (Several experiments have suggested that such women may be relatively sedentary and that they burn up so few calories that they develop a weight problem despite their reasonable eating patterns.) Sue assured me that she wasn't very sedentary: she said she was very tired every evening. I noted that fatigue is not a good index of physical exertion and that perhaps she should look into the possibility that her weight problem could be conquered without hunger pangs, headaches, and the usual side effects of starvation dieting.

The next day she called me at the office and made an appointment to talk further about my strange-sounding ideas. Since we already had a fairly clear definition of her problem and its area (stage one), I decided to move right into stage two (collecting information). I asked Sue for the next two weeks to keep a daily record of the number of calories she consumed—without making any strenuous efforts to reduce her food intake. At the same time, I asked her to wear a digital pedometer—a small device which looks like a pocket watch and measures the number of miles walked per day. After two weeks my suspicions were borne out.

Eating in her usual, comfortable fashion, Sue was consuming less than 1700 calories per day at a body weight of one hundred sixty-three pounds. A physically active person can "afford" about 13 to 14 calories per pound so that—theoretically—she should have been losing weight if she were eating less than 2100 calories per day. Why, then, wasn't she losing weight? This mystery was easily solved by looking at her pedometer records.

Sue was walking about 1.6 miles per day—significantly less than the average-weight woman. The obvious implication was to have her increase her physical activity without changing her diet, and we discussed ways in which she could do this gradually and comfortably (that is, without painful calisthenics or a smelly sweatsuit). After looking at several options, Sue decided to try something very simple—she would walk around the room or jog in place during all television commercials. Given that she had the television on most of the day, this amounted to a considerable number of calories. Six months later, she had lost eighteen pounds and was still slimming—without hunger pangs, dizziness, or sore muscles.

Notice that Sue's initial self-change efforts were way off base. She had assumed that her excess pounds came from overeating (a behavior pattern), and so she had made changes which were not addressed to the real cause of her problem. With a little PPS training, she was able to determine that her obesity was primarily caused by her physical inactivity rather than her diet. This is only one example in which a failure to collect information has been responsible for ineffective problem solving.

More often than not, accurate personal information can be among the most important elements in successful self-change. *It is hard to get directions if you don't know where you are.* After you have identified a problem area, it is very helpful to become more aware of the problem itself. "Awareness" involves more than just paying close attention, however. To be really helpful, your personal information should be very thorough. The more thorough that information, the more likely it is that it will offer clues to possible causes and solutions for your problems.

Let me illustrate with another example. Bob R. had been referred for counseling because of persistent "anxiety attacks." Two or three times a day he would experience a sudden feeling of sheer panic and terror. His hands would begin to tremble, he would break out in a cold sweat, and his heart would start pounding. A previous counselor had given him an ominous-sounding diagnosis and placed him on tranquilizers. The drugs were somewhat helpful, but they interfered with his work and made him continuously groggy.

When Bob came to see me, I first asked that he have a complete physical checkup. In his case, this checkup revealed no medical abnormalities.*

After Bob had specified the problem and established some short-term goals, I asked him to keep a record of his anxiety attacks. He was supposed to write down where they occurred, the time of day, any persons present, whatever thoughts preceded it, and so on. After fifteen days, we began to see an interesting pattern. Some of Bob's attacks occurred at home, others at work. They didn't seem to be associated with one particular person or time of day. But there was still an interesting pattern. Consider the following excerpts from his PPS diary:

Day	Time	Place	Preceding Events
Monday	10:15 A.M.	office (bathroom)	Nothing I can remember; I had just left my office and walked upstairs to go to the bathroom; I noticed that my heart was starting to beat faster, and then it hit me like a locomotive.
Thursday	11:00 P.M.	home (bedroom)	My wife had been in the bathroom for a long time, and when she came out, she was wearing a new gown, and her hair was all fixed up; I remember

---

*Before beginning any self-change project which might involve medical problems, it is a good idea to have a medical exam and obtain the approval of your physician.

thinking that she might want to make love, and then all of a sudden I began to shake and perspire.

Saturday   2:00 P.M.   home
                                 (yard)

My son had gone to a football game, and our yard was really overdue for mowing; I rolled out our power mower, and after the third or fourth tug on the starter rope, I began to flush, and then I knew it was coming on again

These are only three of the instances, but they reflect a fairly consistent pattern. If you enjoy detective novels or mysteries, you may want to take a moment here to see if you can detect the nature of this pattern. We will spend more time on this particular skill in the next chapter. For the time being, it is worth noting that Bob's anxiety attacks were almost always preceded by physical exertion or the anticipation of it. As soon as he noticed any increase in his pulse, he became very anxious (which further increased his pulse), and he was soon the victim of a vicious cycle. Further interviewing and some homework assignments suggested that Bob was extremely concerned about dying and that he was afraid that he was suffering from an undiagnosed heart problem. In our PPS sequence, we moved on to possible solutions, and Bob was eventually freed from his long-standing pattern of anxiety attacks.

What does this case illustrate? Once again, if we had not looked very closely at the circumstances surrounding Bob's attacks, it would have been very difficult—if not impossible—

to find out what was going on and to develop an effective solution. I cannot emphasize too strongly the importance of personal-information gathering in successful PPS. It is often tempting to treat this topic lightly and to assume that one already knows what is causing the problem. Time and time again, however, I have seen people invest valuable time and considerable energy in a solution which was aimed at a mistaken cause.

Accurate data collection is critically important. Notice that I said *accurate* data collection. Even if they resist the temptation to skip this stage entirely, many people are tempted to "lie a little bit" when they keep personal records—to make themselves look a little better or worse than they really are. This may be motivated by the possibility that someone else will read their records or by their fear of finding out exactly where they are in their lives. Needless to say, *inaccurate information can get you in at least as much trouble as no information at all.* Since your problem solving efforts are going to be partly determined and guided by your personal information, it makes little sense to set yourself off on a misleading path. When it is thorough and accurate, personal information can serve many valuable purposes in your PPS project.

1. Accurate information helps to identify causes.
2. It may also suggest possible solutions.
3. It is essential for an objective evaluation of progress.

Embarking on a self-change project without accurate personal information is somewhat like driving a car blindfolded. It is impossible to tell where you are, let alone where you are going. Even if the street is a familiar one, our memories often deceive us, and they are seldom adequate for guiding us in new directions.

What Information Do You Need?

Perhaps it is time we got down to some of the kinds of personal information and how you might go about collecting it. If you prefer, you can think of this information as your personal "facts," "clues," or "circumstances." Remember, however, that at a later stage in your PPS efforts, this personal data will play a role in helping you evaluate progress. At the beginning, the primary purpose of a PPS project is to help you assess the current status of your problem and to develop some ideas about possible causes and solutions.

Now then, what exactly is this "personal information" we have been talking about? Remember that we defined a personal problem as a feeling—specifically, a felt discrepancy between the way things are and the way you would like them to be. That feeling is always connected to a situation, a behavior pattern, or a thought pattern. In collecting personal information, you are basically investigating the nature of this connection. To begin with, however, you have to have a clear idea of what it is that you are working on. This is why it is so important to clearly specify your general problem area (stage one). In almost all instances, a personal problem can be defined as one of two things:

1. as an unpleasant feeling which surrounds certain things you do (e.g., smoke, overeat, etc.) or don't do (e.g., exercise, assert your rights, and so on), or
2. as an unpleasant feeling for which you have no explanation.

The PPS system is appropriate for both of these situations, but the type of information you collect will be somewhat different. If your problem is an unpleasant feeling for which you have no explanation, you will want to focus on your *feelings* and pay close attention to the circumstances which surround changes in your feelings (e.g., time of day, place, persons present, and

Table 2
Examples of PPS Targets

Problem Area	Information You Might Collect
Feelings	
A. anxiety or fear	1. times when you actually experience the fear or anxiety
	2. intensity of the fear or anxiety
	3. duration of the fear or anxiety
	4. amount of time without fear or anxiety
B. depression	1. actual feeling of depression
	2. intensity of the feeling
	3. duration of the feeling
	4. amount of time free of depression
C. headaches (or other pains)	1. actual number
	2. intensity and number
	3. how long they last
	4. amount of time between headaches
Behaviors	
D. study or work habits	1. actual time on task
	2. units of work completed
E. physical fitness	1. duration of a physical activity (e.g., walking)
	2. repetitions of a physical activity (e.g., sit-ups)
	3. arbitrary units of physical activity (as in aerobics)

Problem Area	Information You Might Collect
F. overweight (or underweight)	1. total calories consumed
	2. total calories spent (using pedometer)
	3. "junk" calories only (e.g., sweets)
	4. total mouthfuls (swallows)
	5. body weight (but only as a rough index of actual body fat)
G. smoking	1. actual frequency of smoking of a cigarette
	2. urges to smoke a cigarette
	3. amount of time between cigarettes
H. insomnia	1. amount of time between when you went to bed and when you fell asleep
	2. number of times you woke up
	3. total hours of sleep
I. marital conflict	1. number, intensity, or duration of arguments
	2. critical remarks
	3. positive remarks or shows of affection
	4. amount of time free of conflict
	5. frequency and quality of sexual interactions
	6. feelings of dissatisfaction
	7. feelings of satisfaction

so on). On the other hand, if you are fairly confident that your unpleasant feelings stem from something you are doing (or not doing), then you will want to focus on these *behaviors.*

Table 2 shows some of the more common problems which might be approached from a PPS perspective. Notice that a feeling or behavior often has three dimensions: (a) *frequency* (how often it occurs), (b) *intensity* (how strong or weak it is), and (c) *duration* (how long it lasts).

For such simple activities as smoking a cigarette, you may want to simply count the number of cigarettes you consume. In this case, you are interested only in the frequency of that behavior. With headaches, however, you may be concerned about their intensity as well as their frequency. You want to know how "bad" they are as well as how often they occur. How might you do this? Well, you could rate each headache (e.g., mild, moderate, severe) or you could assign different numbers to different intensities of headache (e.g., 1 = mild, 2 = moderate, 3 = severe). In this case, you would have a bit more information because you would be looking at both the frequency *and* the intensity of your headaches. You would still have left out duration, however. A headache that lasts twenty minutes is more tolerable than one that lasts for hours. So now what do you do? One possibility would be to time the headache and write down how long it lasted. You could, in fact, develop a special accounting system in which you multiply the intensity of the headache (1, 2, or 3) by its duration in minutes. This is a bit more complex than some people want, but it does offer you more complete information.

At this point you may be tempted to say to yourself, "Now wait a second—this is getting a bit complicated. I thought this system was supposed to be simple." It is simple. Bear with me for another page or two, and I think you'll see how it can be very helpful in your own problem solving efforts. So far in this chapter, I have said only a couple of things. First, collecting accurate personal information is a very important element in

PPS. Second, the kind of information you collect will depend on whether your problem is (a) an unexplained feeling, or (b) a feeling which is connected to known behavior patterns. In either case, you may want to focus on the frequency, intensity, or duration of the feeling or behavior. Now, then, how do you go about doing this? Here is where things should start to look relevant.

If you have ever kept a diary, counted calories, or filled out a scoring sheet for bowling or golf, then the next few pages should look familiar to you. In all of the above instances, you were collecting personal information (about your romances, your food intake, and so on). PPS requires that you do virtually the same thing, but in a way which makes it more useful to your self-change efforts. Take a look at figure 1, which shows a sample form of the PPS diary. Most people use one page per day, but you can alter the form to fit your own needs. Note that this is nothing more than a structured form which helps you to record some of the circumstances surrounding your unpleasant feelings or "target" behaviors. By keeping track of the time, place, and surrounding circumstances, you will be better able to identify some of the possible causes (and solutions) to your personal problem. Exactly how you do this will be discussed in the next chapter. Our present concern is the act of collecting accurate personal information.

Whether you are working on your feelings of depression or your drinking problem, you can use the PPS diary form to help you. Simply duplicate the form so that you can carry a page with you wherever you go (in your pocket, purse, or wallet). When your "target" occurs—that is, when you feel depressed or when you have a drink—take your diary sheet and fill it in as accurately as possible. What time is it? Where are you? Who is present? What thoughts were you having just before the target occurred? What thoughts occurred afterward? What actions or events preceded and followed the target? By filling out this form each and every time you experience your unpleas-

Figure 1
PPS Diary

Date _____

Target _____

Time	Place	Persons Present	Preceding Thoughts	Preceding Actions or Events	Subsequent Thoughts	Subsequent Actions or Events	Comments

ant feelings or perform some target behavior, you will be accumulating some very useful "facts" which will come into play in the next phase of your PPS efforts. Figure 2 shows a sample PPS diary which has been filled in.

In your personal recording, *it is very important that you fill out your diary immediately after the target occurrence.* In other words, don't wait until you have a spare moment and then try to recall what was going on. Our memories can be very deceptive, and you may jeopardize the accuracy of your personal records if you rely on recollection rather than immediate recording. If you are working on something that lasts for a long period of time (e.g., headaches), write down the circumstances that were present when the headache started and also when you first noticed that it was gone. The important point here, of course, is that your PPS efforts will be only as good as your personal information will allow. If you start out with false "facts" and misleading clues, you will pay the price later.

Getting a Good Picture

Have you ever wondered why there are nine innings in baseball, ten frames in bowling, and eighteen holes in golf? Why don't they play basketball or football for one period instead of four? Why not box for one round instead of fifteen? Well, there are probably many reasons, but one of them has to do with the concept of *sampling*. We like to believe that we have a good "sample" of an athlete's skills or a team's abilities. If we look only at one inning or one period, we may get a biased view of things. The more thoroughly we look, the more confident we are that we have an accurate picture. It could have been an off day, of course, and this is one of the reasons that they use an entire season of games to determine which teams qualify for such honors as the World Series and the Super Bowl.

So what does this have to do with your PPS? Just this. Your

Figure 2
PPS Diary

Target   Feeling Depressed

Date   Friday, January 6

Time	Place	Persons Present	Preceding Thoughts	Preceding Actions or Events	Subsequent Thoughts	Subsequent Actions or Events	Comments
7:30 A.M.	home (bed)	no one	had dream about being fired	thought that getting up was a waste of time	felt like everything was helpless	just lay in bed for half an hour, ended up being late for work	
9:15 A.M.	work	boss	none	boss commented on my having been late	felt like I deserve to be fired	sat at my desk and couldn't seem to get anything done	
5:15 P.M.	car (driving home)	no one	kept thinking about boss and how little I had done	none	wondered if I shouldn't quit and save him having to fire me	began to worry about how I would support myself	had a lot of trouble going to sleep

personal information must not only be accurate: it is important that it be representative. If you keep your PPS diary for only a day or two, you may get a biased view of your problem and some of the circumstances which surround it. For this reason, *it is important to continue collecting personal information for a minimum of ten days.* This will take you through at least one weekend, and it will allow you to get used to the recording system. Also, it often takes a minimum of ten days for some of the important patterns in your problem to start becoming more visible. Before we examine some of the patterns you might look for, several points merit your attention.

First, if you are like most people, it will be easy to become impatient during the stage of collecting information. After all, you want to get on to the "real meat" of PPS—the part in which you *do* some things which will have an impact on your problem. It may seem frustrating to spend almost two weeks filling out a special diary and waiting for the moment when you can tackle your problem with some active and effective solutions.

The point is, however, that your solutions are less likely to be effective or enduring if you have not invested enough time and effort in these earlier stages of PPS. As already mentioned, many individuals' failures to lose weight, quit smoking, or otherwise conquer a personal problem may stem from lack of accurate information which can lead to misdirected efforts. When you find yourself becoming impatient with these preliminary stages, remind yourself that they are an integral part of your project—and they will help you to develop some invaluable skills for future problem solving.

Quick-Change Artists

A second point worth mentioning here is one which may not come as a surprise to you: *when you first start to pay close attention to something it will often begin to change.* As you begin filling out your PPS diary and recording your headaches,

compliments paid to your partner, or whatever, you may find
(to your delight) that the target begins to change in the desired
direction! Your cigarette consumption may go down, your
physical exercise may go up, and so forth—and you haven't
even started to consider solutions. Generally speaking, the target will change in a desired direction (that is, undesired behaviors or feelings will decrease, and desired ones may increase).
The technical term for this is "reactivity" because the target
behavior or feeling seems to react to the fact that it is being
observed and recorded. (If this does not occur with your target,
don't become alarmed—one of the accepted facts about personal record keeping is that it is "reactive" in some persons and
not reactive in others.)

But what if your target does start to change? What if your
insomnia starts to get better, your weight begins to drop, or
your depression begins to lift? Should you move on to stage
three (Identifying Causes) anyway?

If there is a single guiding principle in PPS, it is that you
should use whatever you find helpful for you. If you stumble
onto a solution that psychologists say should not work—
theoretically—but it does, stick to it. Throw the theory out the
window and use your personal information to guide your continuing efforts. If your personal target begins to change during
phase two (Collect Information), stick to this phase. As long
as your behavior or feeling seems to be improving at an acceptable pace, you have nothing to lose by simply maintaining your
PPS diary and enjoying the progress you are witnessing.

For some individuals, record keeping like that involved in
the PPS diary is sufficient for the changes desired. This seems
to be more the exception than the rule, however. If you are one
of those lucky individuals for whom record keeping is sufficient,
count your blessings. Your target may begin to change in a
desirable direction, and the changes may continue for several
weeks. At this point, however, the reactivity may decline, and
you may find yourself either leveling off or slipping backward.

What is important here is that you realize that this is a very common pattern—it is to be expected, and you should not feel like your progress must end there. Now is the time when you should move on to stage three (Identifying Causes) and utilize some of that personal information you have been gathering.

Some people get themselves in trouble by becoming overly enthusiastic when their record keeping seems to be rendering the results they wanted. When the progress continues for several weeks, they often lapse into a complacent feeling of triumph. Then—sometimes suddenly—the target pattern will rebound or plateau, and they suddenly find themselves puzzled and demoralized.

The way to avoid this disappointment, of course, is not to put too much of your hope in the power of record keeping alone. If it gets you off to a good start and helps you identify causes, it has served its purpose well. Don't set yourself up for a "setback" by counting on your diary to do more than it was intended to. Likewise, if your target does not seem to budge at all during the record-keeping phase of your PPS project, don't worry—this doesn't necessarily mean that your problem is more stubborn or invincible.

At this point in psychological research, we don't know why record keeping seems to produce changes for some persons and not for others. We do know, however, that the reactivity of the target does not appear to be a very reliable indication of how easy or difficult it will be to change.

Shortcuts in Record Keeping

When you reach the third stage (Identifying Causes), you will already have a fairly complete diary covering at least ten days. If you find the PPS diary easy to keep up or you feel that you are benefiting from this thorough form of record keeping, it is perfectly all right for you to continue it. Many people find that the thoroughness required by the diary is something they

Figure 3
PPS Diary (Short Form)

Dates _____   Target _____

	Sunday	Monday	Tuesday	Wednesday	Thursday	Friday	Saturday
Morning (midnight to noon)							
Afternoon (noon to 6 P.M.)							
Evening (6 P.M. to midnight)							
Daily Total							

Weekly Total: _____   Daily Average: _____

Comments: _____
_____
_____
_____
_____

Figure 4
Shortcut Methods for Recording

	Strategy 1	Strategy 2	Strategy 3
	Frequency	Duration	Intensity
Primary Interest:	Smoking	Studying	Headaches
Sample Target:			
Key (or Code):	1 slash = 1 cigarette	numbers = minutes	3 = severe, 2 = moderate, 1 = mild
Morning	//// /	15, 10	1 for 20 min. 2 for 30 min.
Afternoon	//// /	0	
Evening	//// ////	30, 55	3 for 30 min.
Daily Total	22	110	1 × 20 = 20 2 × 30 = 60 3 × 30 = 90 170

can afford only for several weeks, however, and they tend to let their record keeping slide after moving to stage three. This is unfortunate and costly for a variety of reasons which will become more apparent as we further explore the PPS model.

For the time being, note only that *a continuing record of your personal problem is very important for later evaluation of your progress.* When you get to stage six (Compare), you will be asked to take a long and objective look at the current state of your problem—and to compare it to its prior status. This will be very difficult if you have not been diligent in your record keeping.

On the other hand, of course, your personal change project may span several months, and you may not look forward to filling out such a time-consuming diary form as that required during the first two stages of PPS. For this reason I have developed an alternate form, which is shown in figure 3. With this short form, you need only indicate the occurrence of your target by filling in the appropriate box. One form lasts an entire week, and yet you are still able to keep track of such things as which parts of the day are more problematic. If you are interested only in the *frequency* of your target behavior or feeling, you can use a simple slash system for recording. Thus, if it is Sunday morning and you are counting cigarettes smoked, you simply make a slash in the upper left hand box for each cigarette you have. If you are keeping track of a target that involves *duration,* simply write down the number of minutes in the appropriate box. Finally, if you are recording the *intensity* of a behavior or feeling, assign it a special code or number and record it in the appropriate box. These three different strategies are illustrated in figure 4.

Beyond Awareness

There are many popular systems in psychology today, and some of them claim that "awareness" is the key to personal growth and adjustment. In a sense, they argue that persons who become more conscious of their thoughts, feelings, and actions will automatically become happier and more "together." In these systems, awareness is the goal of one's striving. In PPS, however, *awareness is a means, not a goal in and of itself.*

Becoming more aware of your problem is unlikely to be very helpful unless that awareness helps you identify causes and develop effective solutions. You might want to understand your depression, but you probably want to conquer it as well. In PPS, your personal information gathering is an important step, but it is hardly the end point of your self-change project. Now that you have some of the facts about your problem, let's see what you can do with them. It is time to turn our attention to finding the culprits— the causes of your personal problem.

7

Identifying
Possible Causes

Revolution is a personal matter. You create the world; you must
change it.
—PAUL WILLIAMS

As you enter stage three of PPS, it might be worth recalling
some of the points made in chapter 3. There we discussed the
fact that the causes of your problem are the causes of the
discrepancy you feel between the way things are and the way
you would like them to be. We also noted that all causes are
current and that they tend to fall into three categories: (1) the
situation itself, (2) your behavior patterns, and (3) your thought
patterns. It is not unusual for a problem to have more than one
cause, and it is also common for persons to be partial culprits
in the sense of contributing to their own problems. Let us now
apply some of that information to your personal problem. The
basic question you are asking, of course, is "Why do I act (or
feel) the way I do?" As you will soon see, answers to this
question will come primarily from your PPS diary and a little
bit of creative detective work on your part. Before we can
address the question of "why," however, we will need to look
at types of causes and the question of "when."

One-Shot Versus Recurrent Causes

While it is true that all causes are current and create a felt discrepancy, most of the causes we face in our problem solving efforts can be arbitrarily divided into two categories: (a) those which involve a single "one-shot" occurrence and (b) those which involve a recurring pattern. To illustrate the former, consider the case of Jack W., a fifty-four-year-old mechanic who was laid off after fifteen years with a local garage. His employer explained that there was nothing wrong with Jack's work—he was an excellent mechanic—but that the company was experiencing serious financial difficulty, and even those employees who had a lot of seniority were being laid off. Jack's problem, of course, was a feeling of disappointment and insecurity due to his unemployment.

Compare his situation to that of Peggy L., a twenty-six-year-old high school dropout who had just been fired from her job as a waitress. Peggy had a long history of losing jobs and aggravating her employers. During the last year alone, she had been hired (and fired) over a dozen times. Her problem—like Jack's—was a feeling of frustration and insecurity. The *causes* of their problems were quite different, however. Jack had a good work history—his predicament was the result of a one-shot misfortune. In Peggy's case, however, we are talking about a recurrent pattern of unemployment and poor work relations. Both were facing a similar dilemma, but they had to look at different causes and different solutions in their PPS efforts.

If you have good reason to believe that your current personal distress stems from a recent one-shot occurrence, then you may want to move on to stage four (Examining Possible Solutions). For example, if you have recently suffered a financial setback or a romantic disappointment and these were not extensions of a recurrent pattern, then the cause of your problem may have been an isolated misfortune. It may have still left you in a state of distress or disappointment, but your efforts at this point are probably best directed at the options you have for regaining a job or relationship which is satisfying to you.

On the other hand, if you are struggling with a recurring pattern, the remainder of this chapter should be useful in helping you identify possible causes. If you are always failing at jobs or romance or if you are struggling with a recurrent "habit"—nail-biting, nagging, or whatever—the next section will help you take a closer look at some of the factors that may be contributing to your problem. Before we move on to that, however, a word of caution.

It might be tempting to assume that your problem stems from a single unpleasant experience in your life which has led to a recurrent pattern of problems. As noted in chapter 3, however, all causes are current. If you think that your current lack of self-confidence stems from having been rejected in your childhood, you may be partly correct. Such experiences can set up an enduring pattern of thought, feeling, and behavior. Nonetheless, your current feelings are caused by *current* beliefs and behavior patterns. Even though these beliefs and behavior patterns may have their roots in your distant past, they are having their effects in your present—and it is here that you must address them. You cannot go back and change your childhood. You can, however, take a close look at some of your current beliefs and behavior patterns, and you can experiment with some strategies for altering them. Let's now take a look at the process of identifying causes.

From "Why?" to "When?"

"Why do I feel so helpless?" "Why do I overeat? I *know* that I shouldn't." "Why am I so tense all of the time?" These are the kinds of questions that are commonly asked of a psychotherapist. It is very easy to get lost in the question of "why," however, and many people waste considerable time speculating about the possible causes of their feelings or behaviors. One of the most welcome developments in psychology over the last decade has been the realization that there are alternatives to armchair speculation. When clients ask their therapist why they act or feel a particular way, the psychologist is now more likely to respond with a very pertinent question: *"when* do you feel that way?" A growing number of specialists now agree that *knowing WHEN you act or feel a certain way is often an important first step in understanding WHY you act or feel that way.*

Maryon U. had a weight problem. She was about twenty-five pounds heavier than she wanted, and she felt very frustrated over the recurrent failure of every popular diet she tried. Then she came across a book which describes a PPS approach to weight problems *(Permanent Weight Control)* and decided to try it.

After defining her problem and setting some short-term goals, she began by filling out her PPS diary for two weeks. It indicated that she was walking over three miles per day, so apparently her weight problem was not primarily due to inactivity. In terms of calorie intake, however, she seemed to be consuming about four hundred extra calories per day. Now the question became "when?" She had been very thorough in her record keeping, but it still took some creative detective work to identify a recurring pattern. Her meals did not seem to be unreasonable, and she did not appear to do an excessive amount of snacking in the evening. There were a couple of nights when she indulged in some late-night potato chips and beer, but these seemed to be the exception rather than the rule. One pattern which did become clearer as her personal record keeping continued, however, was afternoon snacking. Three days out of four she would indulge in a couple of doughnuts or a handful of cookies right around 3:30 in the afternoon.

Now we had some clues as to *when* she was consuming the extra calories, and we started to look for the *why.* Was she experiencing hunger pangs after a light lunch? Not according to her diary. Did she watch a particular television program that advertised sweets at about that time? Again, the answer seemed no. However, her diary indicated that her snacking was often preceded by the arrival of her two children home from school. Was that important? It turned out that it was. When they got home, she always sat down with them and listened to their reports of what had taken place in school that day. It had become a tradition for her to have some snacks ready for them —usually cookies and milk. By now, the plot was thickening. It looked like Maryon was sharing in her children's after-school snacks, and that her four hundred calories might be coming from a few doughnuts and some milk in the afternoons. We looked at some possible ways to alter that pattern, and within two months she was beginning to slim down toward the weight she wanted.

Note the important role of the pps diary in the above example. Without accurate and thorough information about the circumstances surrounding her food intake, it would have been impossible for Maryon to have identified the causes of her weight problem. It obviously took more than the diary, though, and perhaps we should spend a little bit of time on the detective skills that go into discovering a pattern in your problem.

Starting with the ABC's

Behavioral psychologists like to talk about the fact that any behavior "B" is sandwiched in between the things which precede it (its antecedents, "A") and the things which follow it (its consequences, "C"). Thus, when you are trying to figure out what is going on in your life, you are often trying to learn about your own ABC's. An antecedent—something which precedes your problem target—can exert a powerful influence. Have you ever noticed, for example, that you are more likely to light up a cigarette if you have just finished a meal or smelled someone else's cigarette? These events have become "cues" for you to light up. Likewise, a television commercial about beer or pizza may become just the goad you needed to make a quick trip to the refrigerator for a late-night snack.

Just as important as the antecedent, however, is the consequence—the things which follow the occurrence of the behavior or feeling you are working on. Take the case of your leaving the television set to raid the regrigerator. Here, the commercial was a cue (the A of your ABCs), and your act of walking to the refrigerator was the behavior (B). The consequence (C) will depend on what lies waiting for you in the refrigerator. If there are plenty of goodies, then your behavior will have paid off— you will, in a sense, have been rewarded for efforts. On the other hand, if the cupboard is bare (at least of sweets and snack foods), your behavior will not have been rewarded.

Generally speaking, we tend to repeat behaviors which "pay off" with rewarding consequences, and we tend not to repeat those which have no such payoff (or which may, in fact, be punishing). This does not mean that we are reflexive creatures like Pavlov's proverbial dog, but it does remind us that we are sensitive to the consequences of our actions. If yelling at the kids succeeds in producing what we want from them, we are more likely to continue. Likewise, if our overtures of affection toward our partner are met with cynical remarks or no consequence at all, we will be less likely to repeat them.

So far we have been talking about antecedents and consequences as if they were all "out there" in the real world of other persons and things. Many of the events which precede and follow our behavior and feelings, however, are very private. In fact, they may be known only to ourselves. The vast majority of our actions and feelings are preceded by thoughts, fantasies, and other private events. Except in the case of very "automatic" habits, we often consciously think about what it is that we are about to do. Before entering a tavern or stopping at the doughnut store, we probably have some thought or image flash through our minds. Likewise, after we have done something, most of us engage in a little self-evaluation. More often than not, we criticize our behavior and berate our worth as a person.

Needless to say, thought patterns such as these can not only lead to problematic behaviors; they are also conducive to unpleasant feelings. Over a long period of time, some of these thought patterns may become so familiar that they are almost automatic.

This is similar to what you may have experienced when you first learned to drive a car. If it didn't have an automatic transmission, your head was probably filled with all sorts of instructions to yourself: "First push in the clutch. . . . Now put it in gear. . . . Good, OK, now slowly give it some gas and let the clutch out. . . . " After a while, of course, these self-instructions became unnecessary, and you may then have found that you spent a lot of your time in the driver's seat daydreaming rather than paying close attention to what you were doing. It is these automatic or habitual thought patterns that are often the most difficult to detect, and you should bear this in mind as you search your PPS diary for relevant patterns.

Let's take a closer look at how you can detect these patterns. First, lay your PPS diary forms out in front of you. As you look over the forms, try to get a sense of general differences. If you have to, stand back from the forms and see if you notice that there is more writing in some sections than in others. Presumably, the more writing there is, the more frequently your target occurred. It is often helpful to quantify your record keeping as you search for relevant patterns. This can be done by using a form such as the one shown in figure 5. Whether you are simply counting the frequency of something or you are using a system that involves duration or intensity, you should be able to fill in some summary numbers in each box.

If you are trying to improve your self-image, for example, you might be keeping track of the number of times you say something positive to yourself. It may turn out that this is very different on weekends versus weekdays, or in the evenings as

Figure 5
PPS Pattern Search Form

Pattern

Day of the Week	Sun.	Mon.	Tues.	Wed.	Thurs.	Fri.	Sat.

	Morning (midnight to noon)	Afternoon (noon to 6 P.M.)	Evening (6 P.M. to midnight)
Time of Day			

	Home	Work/School	Other
Place			

Persons Present				

opposed to the earlier parts of the day. Likewise, you may be less complimentary to yourself when you are at work than when you are home, especially if your boss is around. These are important patterns, and they will help you identify possible solutions.

The form provided in figure 5 does not allow you to record thoughts and actions which preceded or followed your target occurrence. This is not because they are less important but because it may be more difficult to divide them into such neat categories. As you look over your PPS diary, pay close attention to any possible patterns involving your thought and action patterns. Are you frequently thinking about a particular topic just before you act or feel badly? What do you do afterward? What do you think? It is surprising how many personal problems are the result of self-defeating thoughts and self-critical evaluations. As a matter of fact, if you cannot find a pattern among the categories listed in figure 5, it is likely that your problem may be related to the thought and behavior patterns which precede and follow your target occurrence.

What if you can't find a pattern? This does occur sometimes, and it doesn't necessarily mean that yours is a hopeless case. The pattern is there, but it may be very difficult to identify. Some of the most common culprits here are the following.

First, if your PPS diary is inaccurate or inadequate in its thoroughness, it should not be surprising if you have trouble finding a pattern. The solution to this dilemma, of course, is to extend you record keeping with more conscientious attention to details and accuracy.

If you are confident that your diary *is* accurate and thorough, then it may be the case that your problem occurrence is either so frequent or so infrequent that it is hard to see any pattern there. If it is very infrequent, your best bet again is to extend your record keeping until you have a better sample of your problem. If it is very frequent and does not appear to be associated with any particular time, place, day, or person, you may be facing a problem which involves automatic thought patterns. Try to look more closely at what it is that you are doing, thinking, or feeling right before you engage in your target. Do the same for the thoughts, feelings, and actions which follow the target. With a bit more snooping and some patient detective work, it is usually possible to uncover a pattern.

Finally, one strategy to use when you are having trouble finding a pattern is to enlist the aid of close friends or family members. Don't tell them that you can't see a pattern. Make it like a mystery game in which you have given them some clues to a "crime" and it is their task to figure out what it is that is frequently associated with the crime. Be sure to point out to them that the "culprits" can either precede or follow the act or feeling you are interested in. This strategy is often success- ful, perhaps because other people can back up from the situa- tion a little better than you and may be able to see the forest as well as the trees.

8

Examining
Possible Solutions

*One person with a belief is equal to a force of ninety-nine who have
only interests.*

—JOHN STUART MILL

There is more than a little truth in the idea that the accurate
identification of a cause is an important step toward the solution of a problem. Since personal problems are caused by a
combination of thought and behavior patterns and situations,
it should come as no surprise that solutions to these problems
will require making changes in one or more of these areas.

Before we discuss how you might go about examining possible solutions to your problem, two points are worth mentioning. First, it might be more accurate to say that your primary
goal is to produce *improvement.* Many individuals become
upset when they fail to identify a complete solution to their
current personal problems. Since many of these problems may
result from a long history of thought or behavior patterns—or
from situational circumstances that are hard to change—it
would not be reasonable to expect them to be remedied overnight. As you begin to investigate problem solutions, keep in
mind that your short-term sights should be set on improvement, not miraculous resolution. Over time, the improvements
accumulate, often adding up to resolution.

A second preliminary point is to emphasize the difference

between "means" and "ends." Means are methods or strategies that are used to obtain certain ends or goals. As you pursue problem solutions, it is important to keep in mind that a solution is always a means—it involves acting or thinking differently. Your goal, of course, is to feel better, but this is the outcome of your solution, not the solution itself. Don't confuse your goal with the strategies you intend to use to attain it.

According to the analysis presented in chapter 3, problem solutions are strategies that effectively reduce the felt discrepancy between the way things are and the way you would like them to be. In chapter 7 we discussed ways of identifying the culprits in your personal problems. Now it is time to turn our attention to possible strategies for addressing those problems. Our discussion will first examine strategies that are aimed at changing thought patterns. Next we will discuss behavior change strategies, and we will then examine methods for changing situations that may be relevant to a personal problem.

Changing Thought Patterns

Several years ago I was consulted by a young Vietnam veteran, Johnny L., who was very anxious: he said he was afraid that he was losing his mind. I asked him to describe how he felt and what made him think that he might be "going crazy." He told me about a series of recent experiences that had shaken his faith in his sanity. He said that he experienced moments of light-headedness and mild confusion and that he sometimes woke up with a buzzing sound in his ears. Psychological tests and a neurological examination failed to reveal any evidence of organic problems, but Johnny was still terrified by the thought that he was slowly sliding into insanity. I asked him to fill out a personal diary of his thoughts and feelings for two weeks, and we soon had some suspects in our search for the causes of his problem.

It appeared that Johnny was more than ready to "see" craziness in almost anything he did. Thus, after experiencing a mild headache, he jumped to the conclusion that he had a brain tumor. He also kept a constant vigil on his sanity, watching his every thought and move to see if they were "abnormal." I pointed out that this constant pressure might itself lead to a self-fulfilling prophecy—a speculation that was consistent with the observation that he often experienced his "symptoms" only after he had begun to worry about them. It became clear that he had become so biased in his self-perceptions that there was hardly anything that didn't seem "crazy" to him. Our problem solving strategy was thus directed at changing his biased thought patterns.

In changing thought patterns, of course, one may be changing not only the perception of events but also their evaluation. As emphasized earlier in this book, we respond to the world according to our beliefs about it. If we believe that the world is full of dangerous and threatening events, we should not be surprised to find that our life-style is one filled with caution and anxiety. Likewise, if we see ourselves as inadequate and fate as unchangeable, we may live a life filled with apathy and despair.

Proponents of "positive thinking" have sometimes gone overboard in suggesting that we create a nonthreatening and jubilant world just by changing the way we think. Changing thought patterns often leads to altered feelings and altered behavior, and this is hardly an insignificant matter, but we must be careful not to assume that we can "wish" our world into a paradise.

The viewpoint presented in this book is basically as follows: *how you think about yourself and your problem will significantly affect how you feel and what you do about it.*

Notice that "what you do about it" cannot be separated from your thought patterns. If you think your marital difficulties are due to your partner's shortcomings, your feelings and behavior patterns in the marriage or relationship will be very different than if you think that you are partly responsible.

Likewise, if you believe that your smoking or eating habits stem from an unalterable addiction, your feelings and actions will be quite different from what they would be if you saw them as unfortunate but changeable habits.

An entire book could be devoted to methods of changing thought patterns. Some of the books listed in the bibliography may be helpful in expanding on the material that follows, but the basic points are the same. If you have reason to believe that at least part of your problem stems from troublesome thought patterns, your options for change are considerable. You could, of course, consider the option of obtaining professional assistance in such a project, and this option will be discussed further in a later chapter. For the time being, you might simply want to experiment with some of the more popular methods now employed by psychologists.

It is not enough to simply say, "Well, I'm going to think differently: from now on, I'm going to be self-confident, assertive, and satisfied." You can't change beliefs as easily as you change the spark plugs in your car. Many of your attitudes have gone comfortably unchallenged for years, and it would be unreasonable to expect them to change without some effort. How then can they be changed?

The most popular contemporary methods for changing thought patterns involve a sequence of four steps. First, *in order to change your beliefs, it is often beneficial to know what they are.* This is where your personal diary may be very helpful. If you keep track of the times when you feel anxious, depressed, angry, or otherwise upset, you may find that certain thought patterns frequently accompany them. Examples from past clients have included the following:

Paula K. (binge eater)   I feel like I have no control over myself—like that first bite just starts an avalanche and I can't stop it.

Charles W. (speech anxious)   I am afraid of what people will think if they see that I'm nervous; afraid they will reject me if I make mistakes.

Pam R. (low self-confidence)   I've always thought I was ugly; that no one would want to be with me and that I am doomed to live alone.

Many personal beliefs take the form of psychological traps that lead to personal distress and maladaptive behavior. Some of the "mind trips" that get people in trouble include the following: (1) goals, (2) scripts, and (3) bifocals (or prejudicial perception). We have already discussed the damage that can be done by setting unreasonable goals and expecting perfection overnight. The saint or sinner syndrome is alive and well in many heads, and it is one to look for as you explore your personal beliefs. A second category are scripts—stereotyped roles that seem so natural that they may be hard to detect. You may be accustomed to playing the role of a harried business executive, a shy secretary, or a dependent mate, and many of your feelings and behaviors may stem from this implicit role you have assumed. Finally, your thought patterns may trap you into seeing things through "problem-colored" glasses—they may distort your perceptions so that everything is seen in a manner that is consistent with your biased view of your problem. Getting a less biased view may require some homework on your part, and you may even want to consider collecting the views of close friends and family.

A helpful exercise in identifying relevant thought patterns may be reminiscent of your school days: namely, write an essay on your thoughts. Write it to yourself and title it appropriately "How I Feel About Myself," "The Problem With My Job," "Why I Am So Nervous," or the like. Honesty is an important aspect of the essay, and you may find yourself writing down things that you would never have said even to an intimate friend. In combination with your diary, such essays can be very helpful in clarifying some of the thought patterns that may be influencing your feelings and behaviors.

Knowing what you think is only a first step, however. If you want to change these beliefs, additional work is required. Step two in the sequence is straightforward: *after you have identified your relevant beliefs, evaluate them.* Do they make sense? Are they an accurate reflection of your world or yourself? More importantly, do they get you in trouble? To what extent are they the culprits in your personal distress? This point is well illustrated in a personal essay written by a former client. Marcia K. was very distraught over the sudden loss of her husband. He had run away with another woman, leaving Marcia without financial support:

> The last few weeks have been pure hell for me. I can't remember a time when I have been so upset. If it weren't a sin, I think I would have actually committed suicide. . . . At Dr. M.'s advice, I've been keeping this diary and writing essays about my feelings and thoughts. Last night it suddenly occurred to me that part of my depression comes from feeling rejected by Bob. It's not just that I am alone and without work but the fact that he would leave me for another woman. Then I began to think about whether it was reasonable to let Bob's actions play such an important role in how I feel. The fact that he left me doesn't necessarily mean that I am unlovable. . . .

Once you start evaluating your thought patterns, the third stage in the sequence is applicable: *try to think of alternative ways of viewing yourself or the world.* In Marcia's case, she began to look at Bob as the one who had acted unreasonably, and she saw some of her own strengths as a person.

In thinking of these alternative viewpoints, it is often helpful to write essays in defense of them. Thus, if you think you are a weak person, you might write an essay defending your strengths. It is important, however, that your essay be honest and believable. Simply writing things you don't believe is unlikely to be of much help.

More promising is the tactic used by a defense attorney in a court trial. Try to find "holes" in your old belief system—elements that don't fit the facts—and then build a case for a different set of thoughts. For example, if you have lived with the belief that you are an inadequate person, try to find examples of instances in which you were "adequate"—times when you survived difficult stress or performed well despite the odds.

In many cases of thought pattern change, the shift is from absolute beliefs to more relative and accurate ones. For example, you may find that what you used to think was "horrible" is only "unpleasant," what seemed to be "tragic" is simply disappointing," and what you thought was "always" is only "sometimes."

In the fourth stage of thought pattern change, you *actually* *"try on" these alternate beliefs by acting as if they were true.* This may seem like it is begging the question, but the principle of "as if" can be a powerful one. You don't have to believe you are assertive (self-confident or whatever) to act as if you were. In this final stage, you are basically experimenting with some new beliefs—trying them on like a new set of clothes and seeing (a) whether they "fit" the facts of your life, and (b) whether they are comfortable and make you feel better. It is very important to remember that trying them on does not necessarily mean you have already bought them; it only implies that you are shopping. If the new thought patterns bring the results you desire, then you have the opportunity to retain them. Otherwise, there are many others that can be looked at.

Since this last aspect of thought pattern change involves actual behavioral exercises, perhaps it is time that we shift our attention to strategies that are most effective in producing behavior change. Once again, we will cover only the basics, but the fundamental strategies will be represented.

Changing Behavior Patterns

Betty L. had been afraid of dentists since she was very young, and her fear had kept her from having some important work done on her teeth. At age twenty-six she was experiencing increasing pain from an impacted wisdom tooth and had to face the reality that a visit to the dentist was inevitable. Terrified at this thought, she used a problem solving sequence she had learned two years earlier in therapy for another problem.

After defining her problem and collecting appropriate information, Betty decided to look at the options that lay before her. She could, of course, avoid going to the dentist, but the consequences of that choice were almost certain to be painful. A second option was to be hospitalized and anesthetized to the point of being unconscious while the necessary dental work was performed. She decided against this because of the cost and the fact that she would still have to deal with her fear when future dental problems arose. In the end, Betty developed a "package" solution that incorporated some of the most powerful behavior change strategies now available.

First, she practiced controlling her anxiety through muscular relaxation—a set of exercises developed to help individuals cope with tension (see chapter 13). These exercises helped her to detect and regulate her tension and gave her a sense of increased control over the panic she felt when she thought about dentists. Next, she practiced monitoring and changing her "self-talk" so that it was less frightening and more conducive to her goal of sitting in a dentist's chair. She began writing down all her negative thoughts about dentistry and tried to come up with alternate statements that were more accurate and calming. Betty's third strategy was to practice her goal mentally—to imagine herself going through the sequence of calling a dentist, setting up an appointment, arriving at his office, waiting to be called, and so on. When she became anxious during these mental rehearsals, she used her relaxation skills and coping self-talk to control her tension.

Her fourth strategy was a very important one: she decided to divide her goal into small and manageable sub-units. By using graduated tasks, she was able to make progress at her own pace and did not have to tackle her problem in one grand act of courage. Thus, she decided to first find a dentist who would be understanding about her fear and who would allow her to move at her own pace. It took a couple of phone calls to find one, but it was worth the effort. Next, she visited the office and simply sat in the waiting room. Betty did this several days in a row and practiced her relaxation skills and coping self-talk as she watched patients arriving and leaving. This strategy also allowed her to be exposed to appropriate models—persons who were successfully performing the behavior she was working toward. After several days of this, she consented to sitting in the dentist's chair but without any dental work being done to her. She again used her coping skills to combat anxiety. Gradually, she was able to have her teeth cleaned and then x-rayed. At this point she felt that her anxiety was at a manageable level—note that she was not *delighted* to be there: this would have been an unreasonable goal—so the necessary dental work was undertaken. She survived it successfully and rewarded her excellent problem solving with the purchase of a new dress and some well-deserved self-congratulations.

Betty's use of so many behavior change strategies is an excellent example of how problem solutions may require a combination of methods that are suited to the problem at hand. Let's review the strategies she employed:

1. Relaxation Training	These are skills that are relatively easy to develop and involve exercises designed to increase the person's awareness of muscle

tension and ability to control this tension voluntarily. Chapter 13 offers specific guidelines for these exercises, which are particularly helpful in cases involving anxiety, insomnia, and hyperactivity.

2. Coping Self-Talk

This is basically a strategy that requires monitoring of problem-related thoughts and images. Your goal is to be on the lookout for intrusive thoughts or fantasies that may be contributing to your distress and to combat these thoughts with alternative self-statements.

3. Mental Practice

This skill is often a very powerful one in that it requires you to practice an upcoming challenge mentally—to anticipate realistic difficulties and to prepare your responses to them. It is important that your mental practice be geared toward realistic improvement: don't get trapped into generating a mental movie that is unrealistically tragic or unrealistically problem-free.

4. Gradation

One of the most consistently powerful methods for attaining behavioral change is to divide a complex challenge into small steps that are manageable. There may be some anxiety as each step is mastered, but it is usually minimal compared to that evoked by the complete challenge. Two things important in the use of the gradation principle are (1) the steps should be very small and gradual, and (2) your attention should remain focused on the next step in your sequence (not the ultimate challenge that awaits you).

5. Modeling

Another very powerful strategy is to observe persons who perform the skill or behavior which you are attempting. Thus, it is often helpful to closely watch the performance of a friend or acquaintance who handles similar problems with less difficulty. One word of warning here is that your model should be similar to you in relevant respects. If you are a dental phobic, don't try to emulate someone who has absolutely no fear of dentists. Choose someone who has a moderate amount of fear but who successfully copes with it. Likewise, it is probably not wise to emulate someone who does not cope with their problems very successfully.

6. Motivation

It is often helpful to motivate your behavior change by establishing incentives—whether tangible or symbolic. An ultimate large reward may be arranged, but it is more important to establish short-range incentives for

making graduated progress toward your goal. The rewards
should be personally meaningful
and can range from special pur-
chases to a simple congratulatory
self-statement.

These are the most common strategies employed by contemporary behavior change specialists. There are, of course, others,
and one important consideration as you search for problem
solutions is to be open to any possibility at all that sounds like
it might bring improvement.

Changing Situations

It is almost impossible to change your circumstances without
changing some aspect of your behavior, but the emphasis here
is somewhat more external. Instead of working on things that
basically come from inside you (thoughts and behaviors), situational strategies focus on aspects of the outside world that may
be relevant to your problem. The case of Jack H. offers one
illustration.

Jack was a heavy smoker who had been trying to "kick
the habit" for several years. He had tried quitting "cold tur-
key" several times but always returned to his cigarettes after
a few painful weeks. Then he attended a personal problem
solving course and learned to collect some information
about his smoking patterns. A well-kept personal diary revealed some very common and important patterns: namely,
he tended to smoke most frequently in a few specific situations. These included (1) just after a meal, (2) when he was
nervous, (3) when he woke up in the morning, and (4)
when he smelled someone else's burning cigarette. It was
not such a cut-and-dried matter that he smoked *only* under
these circumstances, but his personal information suggested

that these were the most common conditions.

In considering possible solutions, Jack was intrigued by some of the behavior change strategies outlined in the last section. When he chose to start his self-change program, he included a motivational component (rewarding himself for cutting back each day) and a gradation strategy (reducing his number of cigarettes by one per day). In addition, however, he considered the four most popular strategies for changing situations:

1. Cucing

This is a special "prompting" procedure similar to the cue cards used by television actors. It is often an effective way of "priming the pump"—that is, getting some new patterns started. Cueing strategies include putting up reminders in relevant places (for example, special cards or stickers on a bathroom mirror, a refrigerator door, or a key chain or in a wallet). These cards or cues may be most effective when their message is positive (rather than negative). Thus, a dieter may be upset by a cartoon on the refrigerator that makes fun of an obese person but motivated by a small card that simply says, "Hang in there, honey—I love you for trying."

2. Situation Avoidance

As its name implies, this strategy simply involves avoidance of situations that get you in trouble. Many people erroneously believe that they must be able to stare temptation in the face when in fact it is often more effective to avoid the showdown. Thus, a dieter may avoid some temptations by not going to a particular restaurant, by not bringing sweets home, and so on. The person who wants to quit smoking may avoid situations that often lead to smoking (e.g., by leaving the table right after a meal, temporarily avoiding friends who are heavy smokers, or asking them not to smoke, etc.).

3. Planned Difficulty

This is a strategy that requires the person to make an undesired habit more difficult by stacking the odds against it ahead of time. The person who is trying to be more active physically, for example, may rearrange his or her office or home so that more movement is required in day-to-day activities. Likewise, the smoker may refuse to carry cigarettes or matches (thus making it necessary to "bum" a cigarette or light). The problem drinker may move liquor from its old familiar storage place in the home to one that requires a bit more effort and conscious pursuit.

4. Social Support

This is probably one of the most powerful of the situation change strategies because it enlists the encouragement and support of other people. Thus, the father with a "temper problem" may ask his wife and children to help him in his efforts—to give him gentle feedback when he seems abrasive and to commend him when he handles a difficult situation without blowing his top. Asking co-workers, friends, and family members to cooperate and support your self-change efforts may be extremely helpful, particularly if your own motivation is sagging. In these requests, however, it is important that they understand that you want support and encouragement— not a parole officer or a parent. Remind them of the old song that it is better to "accentuate the positive, and eliminate the negative" in the feedback they give you.

Because Jack's solutions for quitting smoking were initially less successful than he desired, a more detailed description of his efforts will be necessary, but I shall postpone this discussion until we get to stage seven of the PPS sequence. For the moment let us review the strategies outlined in this chapter.

Summary

We began this chapter by recalling that problem solutions are strategies that effectively change the felt discrepancy between the way things are and the way you would like them to be. This is usually accomplished by changing one or more things: your thought patterns, your behavior patterns, or certain situations that may influence your problem. Each of these three areas was then discussed. When we explored methods of changing thought patterns, we saw that the most popular contemporary methods involve four steps: (1) identifying beliefs, fantasies, and thought patterns that may be contributing to your problem, (2) evaluating those patterns in terms of their reasonableness and their effects, (3) considering alternative ways of thinking about yourself, your problem, or the world, and (4) trying on these alternative thought patterns by temporarily acting as if they were true. In this last stage, of course, you are required to take some action—to experiment with what it would be like to think, feel, and behave in a different manner.

Since behavior change is itself something that may require special efforts, we next discussed some of the more popular methods for altering behavior patterns. Six basic strategies were examined: (1) relaxation training—some special exercises designed to help you cope with tension, (2) coping self-talk—the strategy of closely watching and changing what you "say to yourself" so that it helps rather than hinders your problem solving efforts, (3) mental practice—running a "mental movie" of your performance before you actually attempt it, (4) gradation—dividing your challenge into small steps that increase very gradually in the demands they place on you, (5) modeling—watching how someone else copes with the same problem, and (6) motivation—establishing incentives for your continued efforts and short-term progress. It was emphasized that these are only the most popular strategies—there are many others that could be employed, and you should try to think of as many as possible before you select the one(s) that you will eventually experiment with.

Finally, we discussed the four most popular techniques for changing situations. These were: (1) cueing yourself with special cards or prompts that remind you of your efforts and encourage you to continue them, (2) the avoidance of situations where you are most likely to have trouble, (3) planning to make it difficult to go wrong by prearranging your environment such that your problem is less likely to occur, and (4) requesting the support, cooperation, and encouragement of friends, co-workers, and family members. This last strategy may be one of the most powerful available and should not be taken lightly as you consider possible problem solutions.

At this point you may feel a little overwhelmed with this wide array of strategies and with some mixed feelings about their promise. Some of them may sound rather reasonable for the problem you are dealing with, but others may seem far afield. The point is that there is a wide range of options open to you, whatever your problem. In this chapter we have literally skimmed the surface and looked only at the cream of the crop —some of the most powerful and popular strategies employed by contemporary counselors. You don't have to memorize the options outlined here, nor should you restrict yourself to them. What is important is that you appreciate the wide range of choices you have. Don't pass judgment on them before you have given them a chance and don't sabotage your own efforts by thinking they are too complicated to pursue. In the next stage of personal problem solving we will reduce the complexity by talking about how to narrow this wide range of options and choose the one(s) that seem most promising for your own purposes.

9

Narrowing and Trying

Life is nothing if not an adventure.
—HELEN KELLER

In following the personal problem solving sequence, it is not unusual for individuals to be impatient. After all, some part of your life is unsatisfactory—you want to rush in and "fix it up" as soon as possible. Although your eagerness is very understandable and there is some danger in waiting too long before you begin to take some action, it is also important to look before you leap. A half-baked solution can take its toll several times over—not only by failing to resolve your problem but also by undermining you motivation to continue your problem solving efforts. This is one of the reasons that patience was emphasized during the early phase of information gathering.

This same patience is also important as you prepare to launch a personal experiment. A few hours of planning and thoughtful evaluation could save you weeks of frustration and failure. Successful self-change is seldom produced after only a moment's reflection, and it requires more than a simple impulsive act of "doing something." Just as the engineer, the physician, and the scientist must be ready before they undertake what may be a difficult task, it is important that you prepare yourself as much as possible before you commit yourself to your first solution. In this chapter we will look at some of the ways of getting ready for that commitment and then making it a reality.

Knowing Your Options

First, it is often very helpful to review the options that you have available. Assuming that you have defined your problem, collected accurate information, and identified some possible causes, you should have some hunches about what might produce improvement. Take out a piece of paper and actually write down all the things that could improve your dilemma. Begin the list without looking back at the solutions outlined in chapter 8. Write down everything you can think of and—at this stage—don't worry about whether the options are possible, legal, or ethical. Allow your imagination to run wild and simply jot down the things that come to mind.

This process is illustrated by the case of Jerry S., a young boy who was always getting into fights with several "bullies" at his school bus stop. Jerry was threatened with expulsion from school if the fights didn't stop, and he and his parents were very upset about the situation. Jerry's first list of options looked like this:

1. I could stop taking the bus.
2. I could have one of my parents stay with me until the bus arrives.
3. I could wait in the house until the bus is almost here and then make a mad dash for it.
4. I could take out a Mafia contract on those bums (ha, ha).
5. I could go disguised as a girl.
6. I could drop out of school.
7. I could try to work something out with those guys (you know, talk to them).
8. I could offer to wrestle them in gym class.

The fact that some of these options seem counterproductive —if not impossible—is irrelevant. At this point your goal is to develop as long a list as possible. After you have searched your own imagination, browse through chapter 8 and see if any other possibilities emerge. Write them all down—again, without evaluating them. That comes next.

The Possible, the Probable, and the Promising

Now that you have tried to be as imaginative as possible, you can look over your list and bring your critical skills to bear on the options you have written. First, cross out all options that are simply out of the question. These are often the ones that sound like "Mission Impossible" tasks—requiring miracles, huge sums of money, unethical deeds, and so on. It may have been fun to think about them, and they may have actually stimulated your imagination toward some more feasible options that would have gone unnoticed if you hadn't been so permissive in your fantasizing. Now is the time, however, to begin to narrow your options down toward the one(s) that you will actually experiment with.

Next, look over the list and cross off any options that are potentially possible but that seem least likely to succeed. You may want to come back to these someday but, for right now, they are your least preferred options. This may leave you with either a long or a short list. Continue to eliminate the less promising options until you wind up with two to four final contenders. These should be your "best bets," not necessarily because they would be easy to achieve but because they are (a) possible—with some effort—and (b) most likely to produce the results you want.

When you have narrowed the field to a few promising options, see if there is any uncomplicated way to combine two or more of them. Remember that you don't want to make life more difficult through your solution, so don't try to move a mountain when the displacement of one pail of sand would do. What you are searching for here is an option (or combination of options) that is at least tempting, if not seductive. You don't have to be convinced that it will work—in fact, you may still be harboring some doubts about the whole thing). What is important is that it be promising enough that it just *might* work—promising enough that you will be motivated to try it and to give it a fair chance.

Occasionally someone will have difficulty seeing any solutions that look anywhere near promising or—more often—will see several that seem equally likely to succeed. In the latter case, the decision can be made "by guess or by golly," but it may be helpful to consult chapter 12 for common solutions to this problem. If you simply cannot think of any possible options to help improve your problem, it may be wise to seek some professional assistance. This does not necessarily reflect on the seriousness of your problem or your own adequacies as a problem solver so much as dramatize the fact that it is often difficult to choose a desirable path when you are caught up in the feelings of being lost. As I repeat in a later chapter, there is nothing wrong with seeking a professional guide for your personal journey.

The Test Run

Let's assume that you have narrowed the field to one option or a combination of options that you would like to test as a possible solution (or improvement) of your personal problem. Before launching into your first experiment with such an important subject as yourself, it is very helpful to perform some "test runs" ahead of time. This is analagous to the use of guinea pigs in some drug research, but I doubt that your household pets will offer the kind of preliminary testing that you require. Instead we must return once again to a valuable ally in all problem solving—your imagination.

Sit back, relax, and prepare to play the role of a movie director. You now know the plot. The hero (or heroine) of the movie (that's you!) is in trouble. She or he has a personal problem that is interfering with a full satisfaction of life, and the time has come to challenge this problem. The movie starts with your decision that you have narrowed the options and are now ready to implement a plan of action. Close your eyes and actually try to "see" yourself in this mental movie. Watch yourself taking the actions you have planned and watch closely for details. Try to let the movie be as realistic as possible and pay attention to how it ends.

This exercise may seem a bit out of the ordinary, but it is often invaluable in refining solutions and forecasting obstacles. Consider the "movie" generated by Carolyn H. After several years of marital difficulty, she had decided that divorce was the most appealing option open to her. When I asked her to move forward in time and imagine herself actually carrying through her decision, she related the following fantasy:

Well, let's see. The movie opens with me sitting at the kitchen table. I've decided that divorce, or at least legal separation, is the option I want to pursue. Now what do I do? I guess the first thing is to tell Donald. Do you want me to describe what that is like? [Here she describes a long and painful evening of discussion during which she announces her decision to her husband].

The next day I begin to make plans. I'll need to get a job and to find another apartment. I guess I'll also need an attorney. Hmmm. . . . I wonder how you choose an attorney. I hadn't thought of that. Do you just look in the yellow pages? Wait. I remember Martha saying that one of her friends had just gone through a divorce. Maybe I could call her and ask who the attorney was. . . .

Now then, who else would I need to call? Oh my God! What about my parents! [Here she begins to cry, and we discuss how she might prepare for the pain of informing her parents, their probable reactions, and so forth.]

OK, now it is months since Donald and I have been separated. Let's see how the movie ends. It is morning, and I am waking up in my small efficiency apartment. I am lonely, and I can hear the sounds of the people on the sidewalk already rushing to work. I get up and put some coffee on. There is this lingering sadness about sleeping alone, waking up alone. . . . I miss Donald. As I take my shower, I ask myself if I want to go back . . . if this was the right decision . . . and even with the sadness, the loneliness, the demands of supporting myself, I know that it is. . . .

Carolyn's test run is an illustrative one because it shows how a little forethought can help to prepare you for the solution you are going to implement. On the one hand, she had not thought about the painful scenes of telling her husband and her parents. By projecting her mental movie, she was able to anticipate these events as realistic challenges that warranted preparation. Likewise, it was noteworthy that her mental movie was not unrealistic. The ending didn't have her swept off to Hollywood by Robert Redford. She was temporarily sad, lonely, and struggling to support herself, but she still felt that the decision was warranted.

As you run through your own mental movie, five questions are worth keeping in mind:

1. Is my proposed solution realistic; will I really be able to implement it?
2. Is it really likely to produce the results I want?
3. What obstacles have I overlooked?
4. Is the solution worse than the problem?
5. How might I revise my proposed solution to make it more successful?

The main purposes of your test run, of course, are to help you anticipate possible obstacles and to refine your solution even further. In running their mental movie, many people realize that they have set unreasonable goals or have expected very unlikely responses from their environment. By playing it through in their imagination, they are able to correct these notions and adjust their sights accordingly.

Getting In Gear

The moment finally arrives when you have made all the preparations: you have defined your problem, collected personal information, identified probable causes, examined possible solutions, narrowed those options to one primary candidate, rehearsed its implementation through a mental test run . . . and now you are ready for the real thing. At this point, you may still be feeling some hesitation; some uncertainty about whether you have really done all the homework required or whether the option you have chosen really has a good chance of producing improvement. Rare is the human who doesn't have these second thoughts. What is important here, however, is that you not get lost in your deliberations. The time has come for a commitment to action. If that action does not produce the results you wanted, it will not be the end of the world; there are other options and future opportunities.

"Getting in gear" may seem like a dramatic move after all the past thinking and planning that have gone into your personal problem solving. In some sense, it is—but don't mistake it for your only hope. You are now instituting your "best bet" solution. Hopefully, it will result in the changes you are hoping for. More realistically, it may produce some of these changes, but you may have to make further refinements to get closer to your ultimate goal. Before we talk about these refinements, however, you will have to enter the arena of personal experimentation. Like the research scientist, you have now had a chance to think through your hypotheses; your hunches have been examined and refined, and you finally have a strategy that you hope will bring results. How do you go about implementing it?

Table 3
Self-Change Contract

I, _____, do hereby agree to initiate my self-change strategy as of (date) _____ and to continue it for a minimum period of _____ weeks—that is, until (date) _____.
My specific self-change strategy is to _____

_____

_____.

I will do my best to execute this strategy to my utmost ability and to evaluate its effectiveness only after it has been honestly tried for the specified period of time.

- -

Optional Self-Reward Clause: For every _____ day(s) that I successfully comply with my self-change contract, I will reward myself with

_____

In addition, at the end of my minimum period of personal experimentation, I will reward myself for having persisted in my self-change efforts. My reward at that time will be _____.

- -

I hereby request that the witnesses who have signed below support me in my self-change efforts and encourage my compliance with the specifics of this contract. Their cooperation and encouragement throughout the project will be appreciated.

Signed _____
Date _____

Witness: _____
Witness: _____

It would be easy here to simply say, "Well, just do it!" If you have been impatient to get started, you may need little more than a rhetorical nod to start you on your first experiment. More than a few individuals have trouble actually starting their self-change strategy, however, and it is to them that these brief remarks are addressed. Assuming that you have done your assignments up until now, the next step is actually carrying through your selected option. To help you move forward with it, you may want to actually sign a contract. This is a strategy that is frequently employed by contemporary counselors, and it has been shown to facilitate enactment of a plan of self-change. A sample contract is shown in table 3.

Note that you are asked to specify (a) what you will do and (b) the time period covered by the contract. It is important that you be clear and specific about the actions you will undertake in your personal experiment. Including a self-incentive in the contract is optional, but the use of witnesses seems to be a helpful component and may therefore be advisable. Your witnesses should be friends or relatives who are sympathetic to your self-change efforts and who will be honest and supportive in their feedback about your continuing efforts. Not everyone needs a contract, of course, but many find it helpful as an impetus to get started and to provide some structure for their self-change efforts.

10

Comparing
Your Progress

Make haste slowly.
—BENJAMIN FRANKLIN

Two things are very important before you move on to this sixth stage in the personal problem solving sequence. First, it is crucial that you have given your experimental solution a fair chance—that you have put your plan into effect as completely as possible and that you have allowed enough time to evaluate its impact. Long-term problems are seldom resolved with one weekend of effort. A good rule of thumb is that *you should stick with your experimental solution for a MINIMUM of four to six weeks.* As with any rule, of course, there are exceptions: it would not be wise to persist in a plan of action if it seems clear that it is intensifying the problem or creating other dilemmas in your life. More often than not, however, your inclination will be to give up on a solution too early—before it has had enough time to demonstrate its real potential. Being forewarned of this, perhaps you will be a bit more patient in your evaluation.

A second factor that is very important as you move into the sixth stage is the maintenance of your record keeping. If you want to be able to objectively evaluate the promise of your experimental solution, *it is crucial that you continue keeping accurate and complete personal records.* As noted in chapter 6, your memory is not a very reliable index of personal patterns. Your daily records will be very important in helping you gauge your progress and appraise your experimental solution.

Moving Versus Arriving

This last point brings us to a very relevant question: how do you know whether your experimental solution was successful? At first glance, this may seem rather silly to ponder. After all, you'll *know* if things are better, right? If you believe that your progress will be blatantly obvious, then it is time to reconsider some very basic aspects of human behavior and personal problem solving. It is *possible*, of course, that you have chosen a solution that will have a dramatic and immediate effect on your personal problem. If so, you deserve to be pleased. More often than not, however, your progress will have to be measured in inches, not miles. You don't turn a marriage around in six weeks, and rare is the person who conquers a long-standing habit in such a brief period of time.

This takes us back to a point that has been touched upon several times earlier: that your sights should be set on reasonable targets. Although we have been talking about "solutions" to your problem, bear in mind that *a solution is simply the accumulation of small improvements.* While you may like to occasionally daydream about arriving at some pleasant destination in your efforts, it is important that you remember that movement is necessary for arrival. This is why your personal records may be so critical in the evaluation of your experimental solution. Even though you may not *arrive* at your desired goal in four to six weeks, your records may indicate that you are at least *moving* in the right direction.

The Value of a Chart

Progress charts are not unfamiliar to most of us. At one time or another, we have probably kept a chart of our weight or some other personal target. Besides offering a graphic display of progress, such charts may be very helpful in evaluating trends and identifying new patterns. This is well illustrated in the chart of Warren J., a college student who had come very close to being expelled because of his poor school performance. A problem solving analysis revealed that Warren's problem seemed to stem from very poor study habits, and he launched an experiment to see if he could increase the amount of time he spent studying each day. After two weeks of initial personal recording, he began his self-change project and maintained it for another eight weeks. Warren's project consisted of setting aside a special time and place for studying and signing a contract with his roommate in which he agreed to defer his evening pleasures (e.g., guitar playing) until after he had spent some time on his homework. The amount of time he spent studying each day was recorded by a special clock. Actually, the only thing special about the clock was that Warren installed a small switch in the electric cord so that he could turn it on and off without unplugging it. He put the clock on his desk and set it at twelve o'clock at the beginning of each week. Whenever he sat down to study, he simply turned the clock on, and when he left his desk or stopped studying, he turned it off. This strategy gave him a very accurate method of assessing his study time each day. Figure 6 shows his daily study time for the entire ten weeks.

Did Warren improve his study habits? It may be hard to tell from figure 6. Both before and after he began his self-change project, Warren's daily studying ranged from zero to at least sixty minutes. If he had relied on this one chart, Warren might have been discouraged and given up his first experimental solution. Fortunately, he had been warned

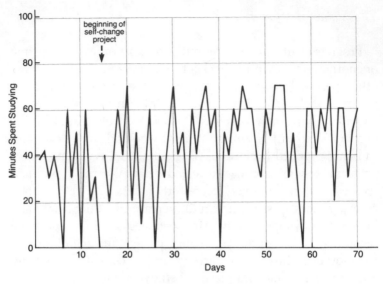

Figure 6

that personal habit change is often slow and that there is more to charting than simply drawing lines. *When you are working on a personal problem that fluctuates considerably from day to day, you may learn more from a chart that uses AVERAGES.* Warren remembered this point and decided to chart his *average* minutes of study per day across the ten weeks. That is, for each week he simply added up his total minutes and divided by seven. The resulting chart is shown in figure 7. Notice that it is now clear that some progress has been made. Despite the wide fluctuations from day to day, it is apparent that Warren's study habits have begun to slowly improve. During his earliest record keeping (weeks 1 and 2), he studied only about thirty minutes per day. After his self-change strategy was introduced, his average went up (week 3), then down (week 4), then climbed to almost an hour per day (weeks 5–8). It had dropped during the last two weeks (9 and 10), but it was still higher than

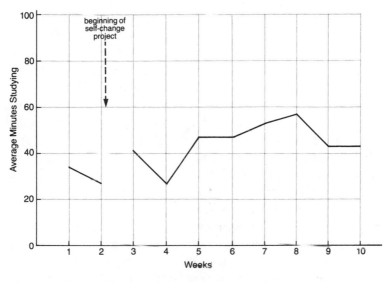

Figure 7

when he had started. This information—along with a modest increase in his grades—reassured Warren and gave him reason to feel that he was on the right track in his personal problem solving efforts.

This last point is worth elaborating—that attention should be paid to the *quality* as well as *quantity* of the personal patterns you are trying to change. Sitting at a desk is not the same as studying: there may be an important difference between the amount of time spent studying and the actual quality of that study. In Warren's case, he had an additional way of evaluating his progress: his grades. In other cases, however, you may need to estimate the quality of your achievements by using a subjective scale.

This was the case with Lynette S., a forty-four-year-old housewife who was struggling with her feelings of depression. Lynette kept a structured diary on when and where she felt depressed, and she rated each day on a ten-point scale before she went to bed. On this subjective scale, "o" meant extremely depressed and "10" meant extremely happy. Like Warren, she fluctuated in her daily "scores" from one end of the scale to the other. Lynette therefore decided to average her daily ratings, and she constructed a chart to assess her weekly progress. For the first three weeks she simply kept track of her depressive episodes and tried to identify patterns. During that time it became clear that she was very critical of her daily pursuits and that she tended to focus on things that went wrong rather than those that seemed to be going right. This probably led to a "self-fulfilling prophecy" in the sense that she became disappointed and tended to avoid trying things.

For her personal experiment, Lynette decided to focus on changing her self-talk. She kept a record of some of the things she said to herself that made her feel depressed, and she practiced counterarguments to focus on whenever one of these thoughts occurred. In addition, she spent a minimum of fifteen minutes each evening writing about her assets and analyzing why she had good reason to emphasize hope rather than despair. The effects of this project are illustrated in figure 8. Notice that improvement was not immediate, and Lynette did not "bust" the charts by becoming constantly happy. No one is extremely happy every day of their life, and Lynette had been reasonable in her early goal setting. She had decided that an average daily score between four and six would be very satisfying and would allow her the normal mood swings (from high to low) that everyone experiences.

During the first six weeks of her self-change efforts (weeks 4–9), Lynette's progress was not obvious. Her average for two of those weeks (6 and 7) was actually *lower* than her preexperimental scores, but she had decided to continue her self-change efforts for a minimum of eight weeks. This was fortunate since her most significant progress was made during the seventh week of her personal experiment. In her diary she

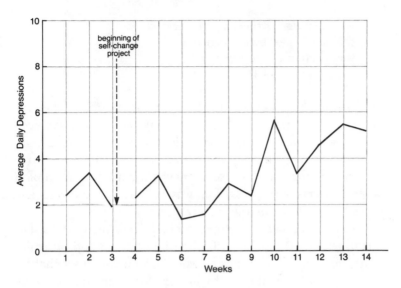

Figure 8

noted that she had finally begun to "believe" many of the things that she had been writing during the preceding six weeks. After a slight rebound during week 11, Lynette's mood remained in the acceptable range for the next three weeks, and she felt satisfied that she had finally struck pay dirt in her self-change efforts. This did not mean that her project was over but simply that she had good reason to believe that she was on the right track in her problem analysis and experimental solution.

Looking for a Change

Quantity and quality are only two criteria by which a change may be gauged. As you look over your records for the period covering your personal experiment, you should try to detect ANY changes in the following:

1. the *frequency* of the target experience
2. the *intensity* of that experience
3. the *duration* of the experience
4. the *patterning* of the experience

We have already discussed the fact that charts are very helpful in pointing out trends and that you may want to use averages when your target fluctuates considerably from day to day. If you are working on a problem that is relatively low in frequency, you may have to use a longer time interval or employ other measures of progress. This was well illustrated in a recent project carried out by one of my friends.

Roger L. had had a "temper problem" for many years. He was usually pretty quiet, but when he blew his top he really went overboard. Sometimes he would become so upset that he couldn't talk and had to be by himself for as much as an hour to cool off. He had always wanted to do something about it,

Figure 9

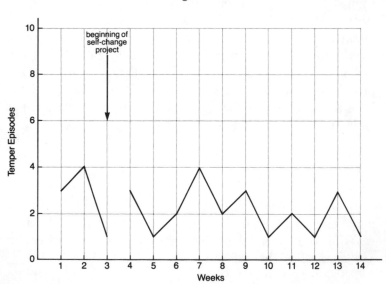

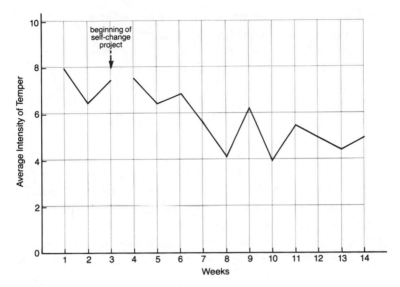

Figure 10

but everyone had told him that temperament was something you were born with—that it couldn't be changed. I offered him a different opinion, and he decided to experiment with a personal problem solving approach.

After defining his problem, he began to keep personal records of the times he "lost" his temper and the circumstances surrounding each occurrence. After three weeks, he decided that at least part of his problem stemmed from two things. First, he tended to keep small irritations inside until they had mounted to a boiling point, and then he blew his top. Second, he showed a pattern of assuming that relatively small irritations were big things—that is, he made mountains out of molehills.

For his self-change experiment, Roger decided to focus on expressing his anger as soon as he felt it and not allowing it to build up. Because his "blow-ups" were relatively infrequent to begin with (one every few days), he felt that he would need at least ten weeks to determine whether his self-change strategy was working. The frequency of his temper outbursts is shown in figure 9. It did not appear that there was much progress.

Fortunately, however, Roger had also recorded the intensity and duration of his outbursts. That is, he had rated them on a ten-point scale ("0" meant mild, and "10" meant very intense), and he had estimated how long it took him to cool down after each outburst. The charts for these two dimensions are shown in figures 10 and 11. Here, it is plain that some progress had been made. Although the absolute frequency of his temper episodes had not declined during the project, there was a clear trend toward decreased intensity and an even more dramatic drop in the duration of his outbursts.

Roger decided to consider his efforts well worthwhile and continued his self-change strategy over the next several months. When I talked to him a year later, he was experiencing

Figure 11

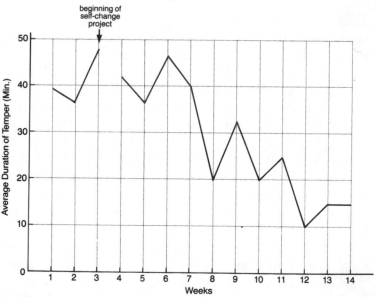

very few temper outbursts and had little difficulty recovering from them.

Summary

This chapter has been addressed to a very important stage in your personal problem solving sequence: the point at which you weigh the evidence and compare your status *after* your experimental solution to your status *before* you began your experiment. It was emphasized that accurate and complete personal records are very helpful in this comparison and that you should allow sufficient time for your strategy to be given a fair chance. Likewise, we reiterated the point that your immediate goal is improvement, not a miracle. Small steps toward your ultimate goal are preferable to large steps in the wrong direction.

As you look at your personal records and translate the information there into charts, you should keep in mind that ANY change indicates that you may have done something important. Ironically, this means that "getting worse" could be an important clue to a better solution. If your self-change project appeared to intensify rather than reduce your problem, this could mean that you have discovered some important factors but have adjusted them in the wrong direction. We will talk more about this in chapter 11. It is more likely, however, that you observed some improvement or no change. How do these results reflect on your experimental solution? What should you do next? Let's take a look.

11

Evaluation: Looking Back and Moving On

The goal of yesterday will be the starting point of tomorrow.
—CARLYLE

There is an old and trite saying that "A quitter never wins, and a winner never quits." Whether or not it applies to all of our everyday struggles, it does capture a bit of ancient wisdom: namely, that *perseverance often pays off*. It is no accident that we have so many slogans that idealize perseverance:

"Success is one part inspiration and nine parts pespiration."
"When the going gets tough, the tough get going."
"All it takes is a little stick-to-itiveness."
"Hang in there, baby."

Unfortunately, many individuals treat personal problems as if they were walking a tightwire—you have to get it right the first time, and it takes only one wrong move to make you fall. This philosophy is so entrenched in our culture that it is often hard to see.

Think for a second about your own past attempts to accomplish something difficult—to lose weight, quit smoking, develop an exercise program, or whatever. If you are like most people, you probably have a history of many sporadic attempts to accomplish your goal. The average American, for example, goes "on" (and "off") an average of 1.5 diets per year. Likewise, many smokers have "quit" dozens of times. For most individuals, lack of perseverance is not the problem: we keep falling off the tightrope, patching our wounded pride, and then climbing back up there. The problem is that we learn very little in the process. Thus, *the major problem with everyday self-change projects is that we fail to learn from our mistakes.* We set out with wild enthusiasm (and often unrealistic goals), and we plunge forward with boldness and determination. When our poorly conceived solution fails, we are crestfallen: we "give up" and crawl back to our old familiar patterns. Gradually, over a period of months, we decide to have another go at it, and we rush forward again—often with the same ill-fated strategy. Once again we are met with failure, and slowly, over time, our determination and enthusiasm begin to decline. We begin to believe that we are butting our head against a brick wall, and we begin to expect failure.

So how does personal problem solving change this? Very simply. The PPS sequence encourages you to expect difficulty and to learn from your mistakes rather than retreat from them. Recall that the PPS sequence is patterned after scientific methods—you are basically applying science to your own intimate needs. In scientific research an experiment is a failure only if it is uninformative. This is also true of personal problem solving in which the results of your personal experiment are meaningful in at least two respects:

1. they may reflect progress toward your goal; and
2. they may reveal patterns or factors that will suggest a better solution.

Let's take a moment now to look at how you can learn from your personal experiment, whatever its results.

Dangerous Dichotomies

A dichotomy is an either/or situation in which something can be classified in only one of two categories (for example, black or white, positive or negative, and so on). Dichotomies can be dangerous when they encourage you to see things as complete opposites when they may, in fact, differ from each other only in degree. This is particularly the case with the results of your personal experiment, which you may be tempted to describe as either a "success" or a "failure." A complete success is very rare in your first problem solving attempt. With few exceptions, most people do not choose a perfect or even satisfactory solution the first time around. More often than not, they choose an experimental solution that produces *some* changes, but not all the improvements they had hoped for. Then comes the inclination to call the whole project a failure when in fact it has produced some important improvements and it may have suggested some promising revisions toward an even better solution.

Before you pass a verdict on the success of your experimental solution, it is important that you consider each of the following questions:

1. Are you confident in the *accuracy* of the information upon which you are basing your judgment (for example, your personal records)?
2. Are you confident that you were *conscientious* in carrying out the experimental solution?
3. Did you allow *sufficient time* to adequately assess the effects of the solution?
4. Were there any unforeseen *circumstances* that would have made it difficult for any solution to have produced improvement during that period?
5. Are you confident that you have examined all possible signs of change or improvement (that is—frequency, intensity, duration, and patterning)?

To the extent that you are not confident about the accuracy of your information and the fairness of the test given to your experimental solution, you must be more cautious in drawing conclusions about what to do next.

To illustrate some of the foregoing points, let's look at the case of Jack H., the chronic smoker we briefly discussed in chapter 8. Jack had collected information on his smoking habit and detected four patterns: he smoked more frequently (1) after he completed a meal, (2) when he was nervous, (3) when he woke up in the morning, and (4) when he smelled someone else's cigarette.

His self-change strategy was a three-pronged attack. To begin with, he decided to use the principle of gradation—he agreed to reduce the number of cigarettes he smoked by one each day. To motivate this self-change, he contracted to reward himself each day that he had successfully stayed below his limit. Finally, he decided to make smoking a bit more difficult by not carrying matches (so he had to "bum" a light).

Jack's progress is shown in figure 12. When he first began his self-change project, there was a dramatic drop in his cigarette consumption. This drop lasted only two weeks, however, and he then relapsed to his previous level of smoking. Since his personal contract had called for a five-week evaluation of his strategies, Jack continued them for three more weeks. At that time he evaluated his progress.

Despite his early success, his smoking was right back where he started—between thirty and forty cigarettes per day. Does this mean that his self-change project was a failure? A waste of time? Should he simply give up the idea of kicking the habit? Fortunately, Jack was open-minded in his self-evaluation. He was understandably disappointed that his smoking was still a problem, but he decided to test the idea that he had learned something in his brief experiment.

First, he asked himself the questions raised above. After some soul-searching, he decided that (a) his personal records

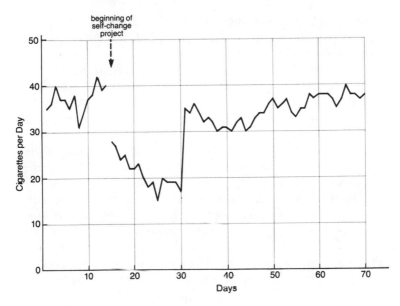

Figure 12

were accurate, (b) he had been conscientious in carrying out
his solution for the first three weeks but had begun to be less
consistent during weeks 4 and 5, (c) he felt that five weeks was
long enough to evaluate the merits of his strategies, (d) there
were no unusual circumstances that could have complicated his
progress, and (e) he had not seen any progress in areas other
than the frequency of smoking.

With these questions answered, Jack proceeded to ask himself, "What have I learned from my personal experiment?" He
overcame his first reaction of frustration and sat down to write
his response to that question. Jack enumerated his insights as
follows:

1. I have learned that quitting smoking is very difficult.
2. I have learned that my standards are somewhat perfectionistic
—I was doing fine until the end of the second week when I went

off my program for a day. After that I had trouble getting back into the right frame of mind. Maybe I should rethink my "on/off" standards.

3. I learned that my chosen strategies were hard to live with. Cutting down by one cigarette per day was too fast, and I didn't really find myself motivated by the rewards I had planned. Not carrying matches wasn't that helpful because there are lighters around the house and I keep one on my desk at the office.

4. I learned that *people* are important in my self-change. When I told Martha and some of my friends that I was going to quit, they just teased me, and I felt angry.

5. I learned that I need to develop a substitute for smoking. After all these years, it feels odd not to go through my after-dinner ritual, and I still use a cigarette to calm me down.

These insights were bought at the expense of seven weeks of personal problem solving, but they were well worth it in terms of their contribution to Jack's progress.

Armed with his experience and learning from his mistakes, Jack designed a new self-change strategy. This time he devoted more attention to its feasibility and practiced it mentally to make sure that he had worked out as many "kinks" as possible. After several days of rethinking the situation and continuing to watch his own smoking patterns, Jack was ready to sign a new self-change contract. This time, however, he was older and wiser—a veteran of personal problem solving. His wisdom is reflected in the changes he made in his approach to the problem. In his second contract, Jack agreed to cut back to thirty cigarettes per day for two weeks, then twenty cigarettes per day for two weeks, and then ten cigarettes per day for another two weeks. He reasoned that this was a more realistic goal than total abstinence and that he needed to feel that he had some control over his smoking behavior. If he later decided to eliminate it, he could set up a new contract. Jack also felt that his new goals would make it less likely for him to feel like he had "blown" his program by having a single cigarette.

In addition to the above change in goal setting, Jack contracted to include three other options in his second self-change program. First, he decided to learn muscular relaxation (chapter 13) so that he would have other ways to relax besides smoking. Along with his relaxation training, Jack started carrying chewing gum with him so that he would have something to substitute for cigarettes when he had the urge to put something in his mouth. Finally, he decided to act on his insight that people were important to his progress.

In his second program Jack asked his wife and close friends to sign a contract that said they would be cooperative and supportive of his efforts. He drew up a special document that was very specific in its requests:

> I, ———, hereby agree to cooperate with Jack in his efforts to reduce his smoking over the next six weeks. Specifically,
> 1. I will encourage him and praise his progress.
> 2. I will not tease him or criticize him if he is not making progress.
> 3. I will not offer him cigarettes or smoke in front of him.

In return for their cooperation, Jack promised to reward each not only with some sincere appreciation but also with a special token of thanks (e.g., taking them out to lunch).

The effects of this second self-change project are shown in figure 13. After spending five days of planning and developing a new program, Jack began with his rather generous goal of thirty cigarettes per day. He had no trouble during the first two weeks and moved on to the goal of twenty cigarettes per day. It is very noteworthy here that he "slipped up" on the fifth day of this phase and smoked twenty-four cigarettes. Because he had learned to be less perfectionistic in his thinking, however, Jack did not consider this a failure but an understandable variation from an overall satisfactory pattern, and he was back to his goal of twenty on the next day. During the third phase of his project he was striving to smoke no more than ten

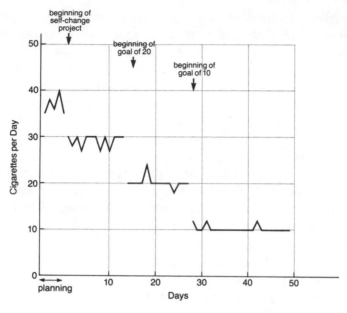

Figure 13

cigarettes per day. For the most part, he was successful in reaching this goal.

Again, it is noteworthy and commendable that he did not allow occasional setbacks to undermine his overall efforts. Because his program was working so well, Jack decided to continue it past the sixth week. He was not yet a nonsmoker, but he had made unquestionable progress, and he had learned that he *could* control his smoking. After staying at his ten-per-day goal for another month, Jack wrote a new self-change contract and successfully kicked the habit for good.

It wasn't an easy task—even for this veteran problem solver —and there were many times over the next year when he had to plug in a problem solving strategy to boost his motivation to remain a nonsmoker. When he "broke down" and had "just one" cigarette at a party, for example, he became frightened that he had gone off the "wagon" and was now a smoker again. Jack realized that these thoughts were dangerous and could lead him back to his habit, so he began a project of personal thought control in which he monitored and evaluated some of the dialogues in his head. Even after two years he experienced occasional urges to smoke, but Jack was then fairly sophisticated in detecting these warning signals and nipping them in the bud. It had been a long haul, but his perseverance and personal problem solving had paid off.

Who Gets the Credit?

Whether your self-change project is an overnight success or a painful long-range struggle, it is important to raise the question of credit. Who or what gets the credit when you run into difficulties? When you make progress? When there is no apparent change?

All too often, people get into the pattern of thinking that progress should be credited to something outside of them while difficulty is their own fault. This kind of thinking can lead to its own problems, of course, in that it encourages despair and lack of self-confidence. If you have tried several different strategies and they have all yielded unsatisfying results, you may be tempted to conclude that there is something wrong with you or that your problem is simply insurmountable. Either conclusion could lead to a decline in your motivation to continue your self-change efforts.

Likewise, even if you have been relatively successful in your personal experiments, you may be tempted to give credit to something or someone else—the friends who helped you, the system outlined in this book, or whatever. While they may have been important, you must realize that they were not the only elements in your success. Without your own willingness to take action and to tackle your problem, all the encouragement and advice in the world would not have made a difference.

The important point here is simply this: *responsibility for successful or unsuccessful problem solving must be shared by you and your environment.* You deserve credit for trying, but you must also take responsibility for exploring new options, making choices, and so on. On the other hand, you can accomplish only what your environment will allow. To the extent that you can make changes in that environment, you can take more of an active role in your own growth and development. To the extent that you *choose* not to change this environment, you are responsible for this choice and its consequences. The most familiar (and problematic) pattern here is to sell yourself short or to blame everything on the world outside. A more balanced appreciation of how the two combine might save you some feelings of guilt and make it easier for you to appreciate your strenghts as well as your limitations.

When the Solution Is Acceptance

Many people believe that a problem is solved only when certain dramatic changes have been produced in a person's behavior. It has been noted in this book, however, that a personal problem is a felt discrepancy between the way things are and the way you would like them to be. Solving a problem thus becomes bound up in the act of reducing that felt discrepancy. One can accomplish this by either (a) changing "the way things are or (b) by changing the way you would like them to be. Both of these strategies are often combined in problem solving projects that focus on goals as well as patterns.

It is important to recognize that you are not necessarily doomed to a life of personal dissatisfaction if your efforts to change the way things are have been disappointing. Individuals who have suffered serious physical injury, for example, may not be able to regain the use of an injured hand or recover their sight, but they can work on their standards for personal satisfaction and happiness. Likewise, it is not cowardly or otherwise improper for obese individuals or smokers to abandon their efforts toward changing these habit patterns and work on accepting their consequences.

The focus in personal problem solving (PPS) is to produce changes in *feelings*. Ideally, one would like to produce these changes by developing patterns of of thought and action that are conducive to overall well-being. There are times, however, when the struggle may be more damaging than the original problem—that is, when the individual may be better advised to work on accepting certain patterns or circumstances rather than embarking on a program of self-change that is unlikely to succeed. These times are, in my opinion, rare, but they are hardly insignificant. A much more common pattern is that of the frustrated problem solver who is inclined to "give up" because a first or second self-change effort has been unsuccessful.

Whether you ultimately choose to change the way things are or the way you would like them to be, it is perhaps most important that you give this choice some thoughtful consideration. If you sincerely believe that losing weight, controlling your temper, or otherwise changing your current life-style are not worth the struggles they would require—and if you are willing to live with the consequences of their remaining unchanged—then you have every right to resolve your problem by altering your personal goals. When this choice is an informed and objective one, it illustrates thoughtful responsibility in planning your own life. What must be guarded against, however, is the tendency to overestimate the struggle and underestimate its possible success. Don't resign yourself to an unsatisfactory pattern until you are sure that its alteration would cost you more than its maintenance.

The Ever Present Option

As you continue your personal problem solving efforts and refine earlier strategies according to what you have learned from your experiments, *it is important to keep in mind that professional counseling is an ever present option.* This fact has been mentioned several times in this book, but it merits repeating at this seventh stage of the PPS sequence.

Human behavior is a very complex phenomenon, and we are far from complete in our understanding of the factors that influence everyday thoughts, feelings, and actions. Some personal problems are more complex than others and may understandably require additional methods of change. If you have struggled unsuccessfully with a particular problem for many months and have exhausted your own list of possible solutions, it is very reasonable to consider seeking professional counseling. Indeed, you would not be exhibiting good problem solving skills if you did not consider such counseling as an option in your continuing efforts to improve your life-style and promote your own growth.

There is an unfortunate stigma that is sometimes associated with entering psychotherapy, but this stigma is more a reflection on the problems of our culture rather than the inadequacies of a person. It takes courage, motivation, and a dedication to personal growth to seek professional counseling, and it is simply irrational to view psychotherapy as a sign of failure or personal defeat. Thus, it should not be surprising that psychotherapists frequently contact a colleague and seek out professional assistance in clarifying their own personal problems, examining unexplored options, and so on. Although occasional jokes are leveled at therapists who are themselves undergoing therapy, such criticisms miss some very important points about human dilemmas. Personal problems are experienced by everyone, including those who have devoted their lives to helping others resolve their personal problems. This fact does not re-

Table 4
How to Choose a Therapist

1. *Where to Look.* Many therapists who are in private practice are listed in your phone directory under "psychologists" or "psychiatrists." Counseling services at a local college or university and local mental health centers may also be helpful in recommending a therapist or in providing services. Many community agencies charge less for their services than private practitioners.

2. *Evaluating Therapist Qualifications.* The terms "psychologist" and "psychiatrist" are usually reserved for persons who have been licensed or certified as qualified therapists. A psychologist has been specially trained during graduate school and usually has a master's degree or a Ph.D. A psychiatrist is a physician who has gone on to specialize in psychotherapy after medical training. In most states it is illegal for persons to call themselves psychologist or psychiatrist unless they have met certain licensing or certification standards. A person can advertise services as a "counselor," "psychotherapist," and "psychoanalyst" without necessarily meeting these standards. There are several ways to check on the qualifications of a potential therapist. In the first place, most qualified therapists are comfortable in discussing their qualifications. Most of them are aware that the different labels may be confusing to the public, and they are accustomed to being asked about their training and experience. You can also go to the library and check the register of such national organizations as the American Psychological Association, the American Psychiatric Association, and the National Register of Health Service Providers in Psychology.

3. *Theoretical Orientation.* There are many different "brands" of psychotherapy, and you may have a preference about the type of counseling you receive. If so, you have every right to ask the therapist about his or her theoretical orientation. Some will be reluctant to classify themselves as one particular brand, but most will appreciate your candid inquiry and will inform you if they feel there is a conflict between your preferences and their own skills.

4. *Specific Skills.* Some therapists specialize in offering counseling for particular problems (e.g., sex therapy, family problems, childhood disorders, and so on). It is quite legitimate to inform them of the general area you would like to receive counseling in and to inquire if they feel qualified to offer therapy in that area.

5. *Fees.* Professional fees may vary tremendously from one therapist to another and in different parts of the country. It is common and legitimate to inquire about a fee before setting up a first appointment. At the very least, you should know the exact fee by the end of the first counseling session.

6. *Length of Therapy.* It is often wise to consider your first session as exploratory. You are trying to assess whether the therapist has something to

offer you, and the therapist will be assessing whether his or her skills are appropriate to your problem. Although guarantees are rare (and should perhaps be viewed with suspicion), some therapists will specify the number of sessions by which they think you can expect to see improvement. Your continuation in therapy is always optional.

flect the hypocrisy of such professionals so much as it does the unfortunate fears and myths that abound about the field of mental health.

In problems that are not psychological, it is altogether reasonable for persons to seek expert advice when their own efforts have been unsuccessful. This is no less the case in the realm of personal adjustment, in which it is often difficult to remain objective and motivated while one is caught up in a compelling life dilemma. The point of all of this, of course, is that you should always remain open to the possibility of seeking professional assistance at any point in your problem solving efforts. Some suggestions for how to choose a therapist are offered in table 4.

Summary

Five basic points were presented in this chapter. First, it is important for you to remember that your sights should be set on improvement, not overnight resolution. Miracles are very rare in personal problem solving, and it often takes several attempts to arrive at a strategy that is best fitted to your circumstances. Watch your standards and settle for reasonable movement toward your ultimate destination. A second and related point is that a personal experiment is a failure only if it is uninformative. Most personal problem solvers do not attain their desired results the first time they are up to bat. More often than not, your first self-change project will produce some changes but—more importantly—it will offer additional information for refining and improving a later project. Be prepared for this development and try to learn from your earlier efforts.

A third point had to do with the credit given for successful and less successful problem solving. It is important that you accept responsibility for your choices but also that you appreciate the fact that what you can do at any time is affected by what your environment will allow and by the level of your current coping skills. Don't fall into the trap of blaming yourself or your circumstances for everything that goes wrong. On the other side of the coin, it is important that you strive to take pride and well-earned credit for your perseverance and dedication to personal development.

A fourth point made in this chapter was that some personal problems can be resolved by acceptance. Remember that your options are to either change the way things are or to change the way you want them to be—or both. For some individuals, it may well be the case that changing the way things are may be too costly in terms of personal effort and likely success. In these instances, it may be worthwhile to consider learning how to live with the problem and to accept the consequences of its continuation. What is important here is the dangerous tendency to prematurely overestimate the difficulties involved in changing "the way things are." Unless you have given this thoughtful consideration and have actually experimented with the stubborness of your problems, it is unwise to accept an unsatisfactory pattern.

The fifth and final point was simply a reiteration of the fact that professional assistance should be kept in mind as an ever present option in your problem solving efforts. There is nothing wrong with seeking expert advice, particularly if your self-change efforts have been unsatisfactory. As noted in the beginning of this book, the program and strategies outlined here are not presented as substitutes for psychotherapy but rather as preliminary options that may reduce the necessity for such counseling. Your options should be dictated by your needs, and you should remain sensitive to those needs in your personal change endeavors. To the extent that the methods outlined here are helpful and satisfying in guiding your personal growth, then you are well advised to continue them. To the extent that they fall short of this mark, however, you should be open to other avenues of assistance. As long as you remain committed to your goal of continuing development and growth, you will find that your options are vast and your progress inevitable. You may never fully "arrive" at nirvana, but you will at least experience the rich satisfaction that comes from the sense of worthwhile movement.

III

Personal
Applications

12

Common Causes
and Options

It is better to travel hopefully than to arrive.
—ROBERT LOUIS STEVENSON

The purpose of this chapter is to offer a brief overview of some of the most common causes and promising options for everyday personal problems. The comments that follow should therefore be read as generalizations that may be helpful in your individual self-change efforts. It is important to keep in mind, however, that every personal problem is in many respects unique and that your efforts are best guided by your personal data and individual circumstances. Thus, you may learn that insomnia is often associated with certain thought patterns and that it has been successfully treated with a handful of techniques. These are generalizations that are intended to help you in the sense of suggesting (a) what to look for, and (b) what options you might consider in your own attempts to deal with this problem. *Do not assume that you should look only for the causes outlined in this chapter or that your options should be restricted to those suggested here.* They are starting points, and they will be more helpful to some persons than to others.

Since your ultimate goal is self-change, your ultimate focus must be on your unique circumstances. Even if 99 percent of all persons with a particular problem were to exhibit similar patterns and similar responsiveness to a particular solution, this does not mean that you have to conform to that generalization. Thus, as you read those sections that are most relevant to your current self-change goals, bear in mind that my remarks have to do with "good bets" as to contributing factors and promising options. If you do not detect the causes suggested—or if the recommended options do not produce the improvement you desire—be careful about the conclusions you draw. These events should not imply that your problem is insurmountable or that a pps approach may not be useful. On the contrary, they simply suggest that the generalizations do not apply to your specific situation and that your efforts are best directed at an intensive self-study of the factors contributing to your problem and the most promising strategies for altering them.

A second point to keep in mind is that the problems listed in this chapter are hardly exhaustive. The fact that a particular problem is not listed does not mean that it is inappropriate for a pps approach. The problems discussed below are some of the most common ones dealt with in our everyday lives, and they are briefly surveyed here to suggest some ways in which pps can be applied to a wide range of personal needs. For purposes of easy reference, they are discussed in alphabetical order. Wherever possible, further resources are listed for each problem area.

Alcohol Problems

Alcohol abuse is a very common pattern that touches the lives of millions of Americans. There does not appear to be a particular personality type that predisposes one to alcoholism, nor is this pattern inherited. The fact that drinking problems often run in families may be partially explained by human learning principles. Specifically, it is common for children to develop the same strategies as their parents for coping with stress. When these strategies are maladaptive (as in alcoholism), the negative consequences are multiplied. Not only does the parent suffer because of his or her problem pattern, but the children also tend to imitate this pattern in their own later lives.

Another myth surrounding alcoholism is the notion that it is a disease. Recent research suggests that alcohol abuse is a *learned* pattern of coping with stress and that it can be more successfully treated than was once believed.

Alcohol abuse is hardly a simple problem, and its causes may vary widely from one person to the next. In terms of possible contributing factors, the following are often encountered:

1. lack of assertiveness or poor communication skills
2. excessive stress or anxiety
3. reliance on alcohol as the main tension reducer
4. a social environment that encourages alcohol abuse (e.g., "drinking buddies")
5. a negative self-concept with the belief that one "is" an alcoholic
6. drinking preferences that encourage high alcohol consumption in brief periods of time (that is, preferences for straight drinks, hard liquor, and so on)

A variety of therapies have been used to treat alcohol abuse. The best known, of course, is Alcoholics Anonymous, a religious counseling group that views alcoholism as a disease and emphasizes honesty, religious faith, group support, and total abstinence from alcohol. The effectiveness of Alcoholics Anonymous seems to vary widely for different groups and individuals. The philosophy behind PPS, of course, would encourage you to explore all promising options and to pursue those that work for you.

There are alternatives to Alcoholics Anonymous and, in fact, some of the most exciting recent research has challenged the long-held AA assumption that the alcoholic is doomed to drunkeness if he or she goes "off the wagon" by having a single drink. Several studies have now exploded the "one-drink myth" and shown that the problem drinker does not have to adopt all-or-none (saint or sinner) standards. Chronic alcoholics have been taught to become social drinkers who can have occasional drinks without losing control. Among the strategies that have been used in these recent programs are the following:

1. Form or join a supportive group that will facilitate the sharing of problem solving strategies.
2. Concentrate on improving assertiveness and communication skills (through a self-help group, private counseling, etc.).
3. Using some of the strategies designed to alter thought patterns, work on clarifying and changing negative self-concept and the labeling of oneself as a "drunk."
4. Alter the all-or-none standard and strive toward controlled drinking that is within socially acceptable bounds.
5. Alter the act of drinking by (a) emphasizing lower alcohol content (e.g., wine, beer, mixed drinks) and (b) slowing down the pace of drinking (e.g., to no more than one drink every forty-five minutes).
6. Practice and rehearse more appropriate responses to problem situations (e.g., being "pushed" to drink); the practice may be either mental (imaginary) or real (e.g., with a mate).
7. Enlist the support of friends and rearrange your social environment so that it encourages more appropriate drinking patterns.
8. Learn alternative responses to anxiety, frustration, anger, and depression (e.g., relaxation training or transcendental meditation).

Two good resources on this problem are *Behavioral Treatment of Alcohol Problems* by Mark B. and Linda C. Sobell (Plenum Press, 1978) and *How To Control Your Drinking* by William R. Miller and Ricardo F. Munoz (Spectrum, 1977).

Anger

In and of itself, anger is not a problem. When you are uncomfortable with your anger, or when you have difficulty expressing it in nondestructive ways, however, anger may become a very important personal problem. Without being able to "control your temper," for example, you may harm someone, lose your job, or unnecessarily destroy valuable property. Likewise, excessive anger may interfere with your everyday functioning and may detract from your overall happiness.

It is normal to be frustrated and angry when you are unjustly treated or are prevented from achieving a legitimate personal goal. People with anger problems, however, often exhibit some of the following patterns:

1. an inability to communicate small irritations (until they have accumulated to the point where there is one explosive and excessive expression)
2. a tendency to perceive everyday misfortunes as personal insults
3. a tendency to make aggravating mountains out of irritating molehills
4. a belief that they suffer from an uncontrollable temper that relieves them of responsibility for their anger

Although anger problems seldom receive the publicity awarded to some other patterns of distress, there is little doubt that they can have serious consequences for their owner. The child abuser, for example, often has trouble controlling his or her anger, and many marriages have been destroyed because of one partner's failure to resolve personal anger. Some of the more promising options for improving this pattern include the following:

1. practicing verbal expression of anger over minor irritations
2. monitoring and evaluating the thought patterns that may lead to exaggeration of the perceived insult or injustice
3. rehearsing self-talk to calm you down in an aggravating situation
4. developing personal coping strategies for anger-inducing experiences (e.g., relaxation training)

Two helpful books for dealing with anger problems are *A Guide to Rational Living* by Albert Ellis and Robert A. Harper (Wilshire, 1986¹) and *Anger Control* by Raymond Novaco (Heath, 1975).

Anxiety

This emotion is a universal human experience. It is normal and, in fact, adaptive to be anxious when something you value is being threatened. Anxiety stems from the human capacity to anticipate danger—a capacity that is partly responsible for our survival as a species. Unfortunately, many of us have over-developed this capacity, and we anticipate dangers that are often improbable or blown well out of proportion. In these cases, we tend to develop a life-style that is characterized by a pervasive anxiety—an ever present sense of impending tragedy. Anxiety is a general, nonspecific emotion, and it is here distinguished from fears. A fear is usually specific to a particular object, situation, or performance. (We will discuss specific fears in a separate section later in the chapter.) Our current focus is on the more general sensation of everyday anxiety.

Most people who experience pervasive anxiety have difficulty expressing or communicating the dangers that they anticipate. In fact, it is not uncommon for them to have a whole bundle of specific fears. The unifying theme, however, is anticipated pain, and the sources of this belief are often found in early experience. Through parental training or a series of unfortunate personal experiences, individuals may develop a generalized belief that their world is a dangerous place filled with unspecifiable horrors and unpredictable dangers.

Self-treatment of generalized anxiety is a very difficult undertaking, partly because successful change may require some very sweeping shifts in self-perception and beliefs about the world. Thus, I usually advise persons suffering from pervasive and nonspecific anxiety to seek professional counseling. This is not to say that the pattern cannot be improved through PPS, nor does my recommendation apply to circumscribed fears (which we will discuss in a moment). However, the kinds of perceptual and psychological changes that are required in this pattern are often most successfully achieved through a supportive relationship with a trained specialist. Some of the reasons for this are suggested by Rollo May in his book, *Man's Search For Himself* (W. W. Norton, 1953).

Depression

Like anxiety, depression is a universal human experience. Everyone feels "blue" part of the time, and many of the sensations described as depression are a natural response to loss. Some animals, for example, show clear signs of grief and sorrow when they are separated from a mate or when a member of their "family" dies. In humans, depression is a normal and healthy reaction to similar loss experiences. It becomes a problem, however, when it interferes with everyday functioning and creates new problems of its own.

There are dozens of theories that attempt to explain the phenomenon of human depression. At the risk of oversimplification, it does not appear that depression is a "disease" in the medical sense or that it is inherited. Like generalized anxiety, it may have at least some of its roots in early childhood experiences. Children who learn that they have little control over what happens to them, for example, may develop a generalized belief that there is no use in trying—that one's efforts are futile. Two of the most popular contemporary theories are presented in Aaron T. Beck's *Cognitive Therapy and the Emotional Disorders* (International Universities Press, 1976) and Martin E. P. Seligman's *Helplessness* (W. H. Freeman, 1975). Both theorists essentially argue that the depressed person has come to believe that his or her fate is beyond personal control. Both the anxious and the depressed person often believe that something horrible is about to occur—the difference seems to be that anxious persons are still fighting to escape danger while depressed persons have resigned themselves to it.

It is not uncommon for anxiety to precede or accompany depression. The latter is often associated with the following features:

1. a negative self-concept and a tendency to be excessively self-critical
2. a negative view of the world and a lack of enjoyment in everyday things
3. a strong feeling of personal inadequacy (helplessness) and a belief that things will never improve (hopelessness)
4. a selective attention to and exaggeration of negative experiences (what is going "wrong" in one's life rather than what is going "right")
5. unreasonable or perfectionistic standards for performance

There are prescription drugs that appear to reduce some of the distress of depression, and many psychiatrists prescribe these as a part of therapy. The side effects of these drugs vary from one individual to the next and are a topic of much debate.

Recent developments in psychological treatment of depression have been very promising, and there are now a number of studies suggesting that even severe depression may be successfully treated by a variety of new techniques. Among these are the following:

1. thought-change exercises that focus on the detection, evaluation, and alteration of thought patterns that lead to depression (e.g., self-criticism, perfectionism, exaggerated pessimism, etc.)
2. concentrated focus on experiences that are enjoyable and satisfying
3. systematic attempts to increase physical activity through daily exercise, errands, and so forth

Like anxiety, depression can be a very painful and complicated pattern that may require professional guidance. This is more often the case when the depression is severe or has become a long-standing pattern. In cases in which there is serious impairment of daily functioning or the possibility of suicide, you should not hestitate to contact a therapist.

Fears

As mentioned earlier, the difference between anxiety and fear is the specificity of the felt distress. Anxiety tends to be a very general feeling of apprehension that permeates one's waking moments. A fear, on the other hand, is usually associated with a specific object, performance, or situation. When society considers a fear unreasonable, it is sometimes referred to as a phobia. A fear of poisonous snakes is understandable—and adaptive—in areas where such snakes are plentiful. A fear of earthworms, on the other hand, might be considered unreasonable by most people.

Whether a fear is reasonable or not, of course, the primary question is whether it interferes with your everyday well-being. Some of the most common fears are the following:

flying	public speaking
heights	specific animals
water	automobiles
closed spaces	surgery or injections
dental work	elevators
disease or heart attack	storms

Specific fears can be developed in a number of ways. Some individuals have had a traumatic experience that leaves them understandably fearful. This is often the case with fear of dentists and automobiles. It is more common, however, for the fearful person to have developed his or her apprehensions indirectly. Most people who are afraid of flying, for example, have never been in an airplane accident. In these cases, the fear has often been communicated by a parent, friend, or the mass media.

Notice that I used the word "communicate" in the last sentence. This is important because it emphasizes the fact that *fears are based on beliefs.* This is a somewhat subtle point because a fearful person will often say, "I know that it's not dangerous, but I'm still scared to death!" The problem here is that there are apparently several levels of believing and what we believe at a rational, intellectual level may be very different from what we believe in our "heart of hearts." Objectively you may agree that airplanes are the safest form of transportation (which they are). At a "gut level," however, you don't really believe this, and your disbelief is very apparent in your terror.

There are several points to bear in mind from the above discussion. First, since specific fears are often based on beliefs, one can "learn to be afraid" by learning the appropriate belief. This kind of learning is not necessarily conscious, and it is often in conflict with common sense. In a fear-generating belief, there is a very strong sense of imminent harm.

These points might be clarified by a few brief illustrations. Individuals who are frightened by storms may not be able to identify the danger that they perceive to be imminent. Likewise, they may not remember any traumatic experiences that were associated with storms. Many such fears are transmitted unknowingly by parents. Small children are often very perceptive and may detect their mother's fear and uneasiness during a thunderstorm. Even though the communication involved no words, the children learn that storms are mysteriously dangerous. Another example of subtle transmission of fear is illustrated by movies and newspaper articles that exaggerate a particular danger. Poisonous snakes and airline disasters make for good drama, and their message is a subtle one: that airplanes and snakes are dangerous. The child or adult who is continually bombarded by such messages may become understandably apprehensive.

The causes and contributing factors in a specific fear may vary widely from one person to the next. Thus, you may detect *some* of the following patterns in your own fear, but it is unlikely that all will be present:

1. an exaggeration of the real danger involved in a situation
2. mental images, fantasies, or nightmares that suggest imminent harm or tragedy
3. self-arousing thoughts that remind you of the danger and highlight its painfulness
4. negative expectations about your capacity to avoid the danger
5. a spiraling fear of the fear itself

This last pattern is a common one in social evaluation fears, such as public speaking. You may be afraid that you won't do well, that you will make a fool of yourself, and that the audience reaction will be devastating. As you begin your speech, you watch for the first signs of your "disaster" and, sure enough, they are there. Your squeaky voice, your pounding heart, and your trembling hands tell you that you are very nervous, and the fact that you are nervous makes you even more frightened! You may experience sheer terror as your mind becomes foggy and you feel your whole body filling with apprehension. (Having struggled with my own fears in public speaking situations, I can readily attest to the pain and intensity of this distress.)

I have devoted more space to fears than to some of the other problems for two reasons: (1) they are among the most common forms of human distress, and (2) we now have some techniques that are extremely effective in their treatment. Despite the fact that fear may well be the most painful of human emotions, it now appears that it can be successfully reduced in the vast majority of cases. Using some of the techniques described below, experimental studies have reported success rates between 80 and 100 percent. You should keep in mind, however, that your goal of "success" should be reasonable.

Few people are ever totally relaxed in a dentist's chair or at a microphone. In fact, there are some experts who argue that a moderate level of fear is actually desirable in some situations. Many athletes, for examples, perform better when they are moderately nervous than when they are either totally calm or terrified. Your personal goal should therefore be reasonable. Don't try to eliminate your fear so much as to bring it down to a level where it does not interfere with your performance or enjoyment.

Some of the most promising options for accomplishing this include the following:

1. Learn a tension-reducing skill that you can use in a fearful situation (e.g., muscular relaxation or transcendental meditation).
2. Using the principle of gradation, divide your feared performance into small steps and tackle one at a time.
3. Form a small supportive group of persons with a similar fear and encourage one another in your self-change efforts.
4. Write down your fantasies and thoughts about the feared situation and then construct some self-statements that you can use to challenge the fear-producing ones when they occur.
5. Mentally practice performing your feared act and, as you generate your mental movie, try to imagine yourself as moderately nervous but successfully coping (by means of self-talk, relaxation skills, and so on).

One of the best self-change books in this area is *Don't Be Afraid* by Gerald Rosen (Spectrum, 1976). Remember that your goal is improvement, not relaxed stupor, and rest assured that your chances for attaining satisfactory improvement are very good.

Headaches

Because there are many different kinds of headaches, you are well advised to consult your physician before assuming that it is something you can handle by yourself. If a medical examination fails to reveal a cause, you could be suffering from allergy, eyestrain, migraine, or muscular tension. An eye examination can reveal whether eyestrain is a culprit, and your physician will be able to identify signs of allergy or migraine. It is not unusual, however, for everyday headaches to be caused or intensified by personal patterns of thought and behavior. Recent research in medical psychology has suggested that frequent headaches are often associated with the following patterns:

1. excessive tension in the muscles of the forehead, jaw, and neck
2. frequent and excessive worrying about matters of efficiency, finance, or time
3. thought patterns that encourage feelings of anger, frustration, or anxiety
4. behavior patterns that are excessively hurried or frantic

Persons exhibiting these patterns have reported reductions in the frequency, intensity, and duration of headaches when they have employed one or more of the following options:

1. daily practice of tension-reducing exercises such as meditation and muscular relaxation (the exercises should place particular emphasis on sensations in the forehead, jaw, and neck)
2. monitoring and alteration of thought patterns that involve worrying or lead to feelings of anger, frustration, or anxiety
3. alteration of daily schedules so that frantic behavior patterns are not necessary
4. cueing strategies that remind you to slow down and execute daily chores in a more relaxed fashion

Your own personal records are very important in identifying contributing factors to your headaches. As you develop a self-change strategy, remember to look for improvement not only in the frequency of headaches but also in their intensity and duration.

Obesity

Obesity is a very common personal problem, and there are hundreds of popular approaches to its treatment. Many of these involve drastic diets that force you to alter your food intake in a very dramatic fashion. Unfortunately, although many of these diets may yield short-term success, most have been outright failures when it comes to permanent weight control. Before we discuss the more promising options, however, let's take a moment to examine the causes of obesity.

Many people believe that their weight problem has been inherited or that they have a metabolic problem that prevents them from losing weight. Current scientific knowledge suggests that obesity tends to run in families but that it is not inherited. What appears to be transmitted from parent to child is not "fat genes" but learned attitudes and behavior patterns that encourage obesity. Likewise, although some weight problems may involve a metabolic disturbance, this appears to be extremely rare. Don't diagnose yourself as a metabolic misfit until you have undergone the required medical tests for such a diagnosis.

Equally misleading is the myth that some people are suffering from an incurable addiction that makes them a "foodaholic" or a "sweetaholic." Although it is possible for people to become psychologically dependent on food, it is also clear that this dependency can be overcome. If obesity were truly incurable, we would not see people losing as much as two-hundred pounds and maintaining that loss for the remainder of their lives. It is true that such losses are rare—it is equally true that permanent weight control is a difficult undertaking—but it is patently false that most weight problems are hopeless.

The fundamental cause of obesity is an energy imbalance—the obese individual is consuming more calories than he or she is spending. Patterns of food intake and energy expenditure are, of course, behavior patterns, but they are often encouraged by environmental cues and thought patterns. There is no such thing as an "obese personality," and the circumstances surrounding a weight problem are extremely varied. Some of the most common patterns include the following:

1. a firm belief that one is destined to be fat and that any attempt to lose weight is hopeless
2. a relatively sedentary life-style
3. eating preferences that involve large quantities of food or high-calorie foods
4. binge eating, frequently in the evening
5. feelings of guilt associated with eating
6. a strong reluctance to waste food
7. a tendency to eat as a means of coping with such feelings as anxiety, depression, and boredom

Many of the popular reducing aids in our culture have been shown to be less than dazzling in their effectiveness. Thus, appetite suppressants, reducing belts, and a wide range of "miraculous" gadgets have failed to demonstrate any significant impact on weight problems. Some of the most promising options for weight control focus on the alteration of one or more of the patterns mentioned above. They include:

1. monitoring and altering thought patterns that undermine motivation or encourage unrealistic goals (such as a drastic diet)
2. gradually increasing daily physical activity through *comfortable* changes in life-style (such as using stairs versus elevators, taking short daily walks, and rearranging office furniture to encourage more frequent energy expenditure)

3. if calorie intake appears to be excessive (that is, greater than thirteen to fifteen calories per pound of current body weight), reducing food calories very gradually by making small *comfortable* changes that do not require total elimination of a food group or drastic alteration of life-style

4. changing eating style to slow down the rate of food consumption (for example, by increasing the interval between bites and delaying second helpings for twenty minutes)

5. enlisting the support of family and friends

6. experimenting with lower calorie foods that could substitute for those previously preferred

7. if emotional eating is a problem, practicing relaxation exercises as an alternate coping strategy

The permanence of weight control is a very important issue since many individuals lose and regain many pounds per year by following drastic short-term diets. One of the problems with these diets is that they are often doomed to failure by their drastic nature. Few people want to go through life eating only cottage cheese, fish, and vegetables. After several weeks on such a restrictive diet the average person gives up and returns to old patterns of eating and activity—the original culprits. If these patterns are gradually changed through comfortable alterations in a life-style, however, the individual has a much better chance of maintaining the loss. Generally speaking, the more rapid a weight loss, the more likely the relapse.

Even though obesity always involves an energy imbalance, the causes of that imbalance may vary from one person to the next. This makes it all the more important to adopt an individualized PPS approach. Such an approach is offered in *Permanent Weight Control* by myself and Kathryn Mahoney (W. W. Norton, 1976).

Sexual Problems

The most common sexual problems experienced by males are premature ejaculation and impotence. Rare is the man who has *never* ejaculated earlier than he would have liked or who has not been occasionally unresponsive to sexual stimulation. In females, the most common sexual problems are failure to experience orgasm and dyspareunia (painful or unpleasant intercourse). Once again, it would be inaccurate to label yourself as having a sexual problem if you experience these difficulties only occasionally. When they have become the rule rather than the exception, however, your concern may be warranted.

As with many other forms of distress, sexual problems vary widely in their causes from one person to the next. A male may ejaculate prematurely, for example, because he is tired or has not had sex recently, or is distracted. Some of the most common patterns present in sexual problems include the following:

1. puritanical attitudes toward sex
2. nervous tension during sexual activities
3. misinformation about healthy sexual functioning
4. excessive concern over the adequacy of one's performance as a sex partner
5. difficulties in intimate communication

Preorgasmic women may benefit from some of the self-change exercises outlined in *Becoming Orgasmic* by Julia Heiman, Leslie LoPiccolo, and Joseph LoPiccolo (Spectrum, 1977). Because sexual problems often require training in communication skills, however, many individuals find it helpful to work with a qualified sex therapist. When this is not possible, improvements may be sought by using a PPS approach that is particularly geared to identification and change of negative attitudes, irrational beliefs, and sexual performance fears.

Sleep Disturbances

The most common sleep disturbance is insomnia—an inability to fall asleep quickly. Other problems include early waking and poor quality sleep. Although researchers have only recently begun to understand some of the factors that affect our sleep, it is now apparent that millions of Americans experience sleeping difficulties. The causes of these difficulties are still being examined, but some of the most likely culprits are the following:

1. Many persons with sleep difficulties experience difficulty "shutting off their thoughts" at bedtime.
2. Caffeine and other stimulants may be a factor.
3. Excessive muscle tension is apparent in some insomniacs.
4. Sleeping pills—bought both by prescription and over the counter—have been shown to actually intensify many sleep problems.
5. Some individuals experience sixty- to ninety-minute cycles during which there is a peak time of readiness to fall asleep and other times when it is very difficult to fall asleep.

Several researchers have recently reported a variety of techniques that have aided persons with sleep disturbances. As with any other problem, you are wise to select a strategy based on your own patterns and likely causes. Among the options you may want to consider are the following:

1. Learn to relax your muscles.
2. Learn to meditate or otherwise control your thoughts at bedtime.
3. Lie down *only* if you are sleepy (that is, at the peak point in your readiness cycle).
4. If you are not asleep fifteen minutes after you have gone to bed, get up and stay up until you feel sleepy.

5. Do not take naps during the day and do not allow yourself to "sleep in" no matter how late it was when you went to bed.
6. Use your bed only for sleeping and sexual activities—do not associate the bed with reading, television viewing, or the like.

A helpful book that uses a PPS approach to sleep difficulties is *How To Sleep Better* by Thomas J. Coates and Carl E. Thoresen (Spectrum, 1977).

Smoking

Although the dangers of smoking are now very clear, millions of Americans have repeatedly failed in their attempts to kick the habit. The situation is hardly hopeless, however, and there is an increasing number of ex-smokers who can attest to the fact that success is possible. Before examining some of the most promising methods for quitting, however, we should discuss some of the reasons for the stubborness of this pattern. Why is it that so many well-intentioned people fail in their attempts to quit smoking? The reasons are probably many, but the following factors have been most often implicated:

1. There is evidence that nicotine may actually be an addicting drug so that the reforming smoker may experience uncomfortable withdrawal pains; these pains are not usually severe, however, and they disappear rapidly.
2. Our culture is one which encourages smoking by making it easy to do; the person who is trying to quit must face daily confrontations with cigarette machines, smoking friends, and so on.
3. Many smokers believe that they will be one of the lucky few who escape lung cancer and heart disease.
4. Many smokers believe that they have no choice—that they lack the motivation or willpower to give up their habit.

A variety of strategies has been employed in efforts to help individuals quit smoking. Pills containing nicotine have not been shown to be very promising. One recent strategy that has received some publicity is called "rapid smoking." It requires the smoker to sit in a small, poorly ventilated room and smoke three or more cigarettes in rapid succession—usually with only six seconds in between puffs. This procedure highlights the aversiveness of smoking, and many individuals become nauseous during the exercise. Recent studies have suggested the possibility that the rapid smoking procedure may cause brief irregularities in heartbeat, however, and it might be wise to consider it as an option only if a physician's approval is obtained. Other promising methods for kicking the habit include the following:

1. Enlist the support of family and friends; request that they not smoke in your presence.
2. Calculate the average time you take between cigarettes and then put yourself on a schedule using a parking meter timer; allow yourself to smoke only when your timer sounds and then gradually increase the interval between cigarettes.
3. Restrict your smoking to certain times or places and then gradually eliminate these (one by one).
4. Set your sights on controlled smoking rather than total abstinence; the most dangerous risks of smoking seem to decline rapidly once you have dropped to less than twelve cigarettes per day.
5. Identify and alter some of your self-defeating thoughts about your ability to quit.

One of the most important elements in a successful self-change project on smoking may be your preparation for possible relapse. No matter how well you plan your program, it is very likely that you will not meet all of your goals and that you will have an occasional "illegitimate" smoke. Be prepared for this and don't fall into the saint or sinner trap of believing that one cigarette makes you a fallen angel. Don't sell out your hard-won improvements because of perfectionistic standards. A self-help guide to quitting smoking is offered by Brian G. Danaher and Edward Lichtenstein in *How To Become An Ex-Smoker* (Spectrum, 1978).

Study Habits

Poor study habits may be a product of a poor study environment, inefficient behavior patterns, self-defeating attitudes, or a combination of all of these. Whatever their cause, there are now a number of research studies suggesting that study habits can often be dramatically improved. Among the most promising strategies for self-change have been the following:

1. Set up a study area that is free of distractions and that is devoted *only* to studying.
2. Keep track of study time and chart your progress.
3. If you begin to daydream or pursue some irrelevant task, leave your study area immediately.
4. Set up specific times to study.
5. Study in small units of time or material (e.g., thirty minutes or ten pages).
6. Establish reasonable goals for gradually increasing your study time.
7. Enlist the support and cooperation of family members or friends.
8. Contract to reward yourself for short-term progress.

Organization and encouragement seem to be key elements in the success of many study improvement projects. Bear in mind that your progress may seem slow at first but that its benefits will be apparent in the near future.

Summary

This chapter has offered a brief overview of some of the most common personal problems, their possible causes and most promising options. Let me reiterate that the ultimate factor in deciding upon your own program of self-change should be your personal records and expectations about the likely success of a given option. As pointed out earlier, the causes and options mentioned in this chapter are generalizations from experimental studies on large groups of people. The proof of the pudding, however, rests in their relevance to your own problem, and it should be clear that your personal records and PPS skills must address your own circumstances as uniquely challenging.

13

Fundamental Skills

The reason why worry kills more people than work is that more people worry than work.
—ROBERT FROST

Many of the promising options suggested in chapter 12 involved combinations of some of the strategies briefly outlined in chapter 8. While some of those strategies do not require further description, others may be clarified by more specific instructions. In this chapter I will elaborate on some of the fundamental skills that may be required for successful execution of various options. Let us being with relaxation training.

Relaxation Skills

Since muscular tension is an important component in a wide range of personal problems, the ability to detect and reduce this tension can be a valuable self-change skill. This skill may be acquired through a variety of meditational exercises, but it can also be developed through a relatively simple procedure called "muscular relaxation training." Originally developed by Edmund Jacobson in the 1930s, these exercises have been extensively studied and found to be very effective in reducing nervous tension.

They initially require you to tense specific muscles and to

concentrate on the sensations produced. This increases your ability to identify such tension when it occurs in everyday situations. After you have maintained tension in a specific muscle for several seconds, you are instructed to relax it and allow it to return to a normal unflexed state. This produces a very different (and pleasant) sensation which becomes your goal in relaxation. Immediately after it has been intensely flexed, a muscle tends to relax more than usual, and this provides you with the opportunity to experience very pleasant sensations of deep muscle relaxation. The experience has been compared to the sensations you feel in a very warm bath after extremely strenuous physical exercise. Eventually you learn to detect tension without flexing the muscles, and, after only a few practice sessions, most people develop the ability to reduce that tension by simply concentrating on the more pleasant sensation of relaxation.

Scientific measures of muscle tension have shown that these exercises do, indeed, reduce the nerve impulses to the muscles, and relaxation skills have been shown to help people successfully deal with problems ranging from insomnia to a variety of fears.

For the greatest effectiveness, the exercises described below should be read to you very slowly by a friend or spouse. An alternative would be to tape-record them so that they can be played back whenever you desire. You can, of course, record them yourself. This eliminates the need for you to read the exercises each time you practice. Reading may distract your attention and reduce the degree of relaxation attained.

In going through the exercises, use voice quality and volume to contrast relaxation with tension. That is, when you are instructed to tense a muscle, the instruction should be given in a relatively loud, high-pitched voice. Instructions to relax should first be given loudly and later in a softer, lower-pitched voice. To assist you or your helper in this distinction, *italics indicate where a soft, soothing voice should be used.*

The full list of exercises takes about thirty to forty minutes. If you finish before then, your pacing is probably too fast. Practice the exercises once per day for five days. Then try to abbreviate them so that you can relax in a shorter period of time without having to tense all of the muscles in the original exercises. With two weeks of daily practice you should be able to relax yourself in a few minutes without having to tense any muscles at all.

Before you begin these exercises, find a comfortable chair or place to lie down. It should be relatively quiet and only dimly lighted. Remove any tight pieces of clothing such as your shoes. If you wear glasses or contact lenses, they should be removed. Dentures should also be removed, and you should try to assume a position which is as comfortable as possible for you. Sitting in a lounge chair, or lying on a couch or bed is ideal. If you like, however, it will be sufficient to sit in an easy chair.

When you do assume a comfortable position, make sure that you are supporting as little of your body as possible. That is, let the bed or chair or couch hold as much of your weight as it can. You don't want to have to hold your head up with your neck muscles, and you don't want to be slouching in a chair so that the muscles in your lower back will become sore.

Once you have assumed a comfortable position, we can begin exercising some of the muscle groups and training you to become familiar with the signs of anxiety and muscular tension. In addition, you will learn how to turn on a relaxed sensation in your muscles. We will do this by first tensing and then relaxing some of the major muscles in your body. You will be asked to tense them and to concentrate on the tension for two to three seconds. You will then be told to relax them. When the word "relax" is uttered, you should immediately let the muscles become as limp as possible and focus on the sensations which you then feel. This will allow you to become more familiar with what it feels like to be muscularly tense and anxious. You will also gain skills in being able to detect these cues and to change the muscular tension into a form of relaxation.

To begin, clench your right fist as tight as you possibly can. Clench the fist until you feel the tension in your fingers and along the knuckles. Hold that tension. You should be tensing it so tight that your hand is almost shaking. Concentrate on that tension, hold it there, and now RELAX and *let your fingers drop very limply. They will passively stretch out and lengthen. You will feel the muscles loosen up. Focus on the sensation of relaxation which you now feel in your right hand. There is a warm soothing sensation as the muscles relax, and you should contrast that relaxing sensation to the tension.* Remaining as relaxed as possible in other parts of your body, again tense your right fist. Clench the fist as tightly as possible. Concentrate on the tension. Hold it there . . . hold it . . . and RELAX. *Let the hand go limp. Now concentrate on that relaxed sensation. It is that warm, soothing, relaxed feeling that you would like to overtake your entire body.*

This time we are going to clench both fists at the same time. Clench both your right and left hands as tightly as you can. Concentrate on the tension. Tighter . . . tighter . . . and RELAX. *Let both hands go limp; let the fingers stretch out very passively. You will feel a warm, soothing sensation. Now focus on what it feels like to have your hands as relaxed as possible.*

At different times throughout these exercises you will be asked to take a deep breath. When requested, inhale as deeply as possible, hold your breath for about one second, and then exhale very, very slowly at your own pace. As you exhale slowly, you should try to relax as much as possible. Try to relax even deeper and let the air out as gradually as you can. All right . . . take a deep breath —as deep as you can. Hold it for one second . . . *and now exhale very, very slowly. As you exhale you want to RELAX as much as you can. Very relaxed . . . let the muscles go.*

We are now going to move up to the arm into some of the other major muscles. As we move on to these other muscle groups, you should try to keep your hands and wrists as relaxed as you possibly can. The next muscles that we are going to work on are in the forearm. Your arms should be lying very comfortably at your sides. If you are sitting in a chair, they may be resting either on your lap or on the arms of the chair. We are going to begin by exercising some of the muscles in the front of your forearm. To do this, keep your fingers relaxed but bend both of your hands at the wrist so that your palms are facing away from you. Pull your fingers toward your face and concentrate on the sensations in your forearms. Focus on that tension . . . hold them . . . and RELAX. *Let your hands resume a comfortable position. Now focus on that warm, relaxed feeling in your wrists and forearms. Very relaxed . . . very soothing.*

We are now going to work on the opposing muscle group in the forearm. Again, keep your fingers as relaxed as possible. This time bend both hands at the wrist so that the palms are facing toward you. Pull your fingers in toward your body. Concentrate on the tension in the outer part of your forearm. Pull those fingers in. Hold it there . . . and RELAX. *Let the hands resume a normal, comfortable position. Allow the muscles to lengthen very slowly.* RELAX. *Very passive. Focus your attention on that warm, soothing feeling in the forearm muscles.*

We can now move on to the muscles in the upper arm. We will first work on the biceps, the large muscle in the front of your upper arm. Let's begin by exercising your right arm only. Leave your left arm as relaxed as possible and try to maintain relaxed feelings in the fingers and forearms of both arms. Bend your right arm at the elbow so that you are bringing your hand up toward your shoulder. Make a muscle with your biceps. To do that you may actually have to touch your shoulder with your hand, but you should feel tension in the upper part of your arm, the front of your arm. Concentrate on that tension . . . tense the biceps . . . and RELAX. *Let your arm resume a normal, comfortable position. It should fall very limply and lightly. The relaxed feeling in your right biceps should be very noticeable.* Remember to keep your forearms and fingers as relaxed as possible as you go through these upper arm exercises.

This time let's do it with your left arm. Bend your left arm at the elbow so that your left hand is almost touching your shoulder. Concentrate on flexing the left biceps. Concentrate on the tension . . . holditthere...andRELAX.*Let your arm resume a comfortable position. Very relaxed. Focus your attention on that warm, soothing sensation in the muscle. You would like that sensation to spread throughout your arms and eventually throughout the rest of your body.*

Let's go back to the right arm again. This time we will be exercising the triceps muscle, which is the back part of your upper arm. In order to flex this muscle you have to straighten your arm out. You should try to keep your wrist and forearm as relaxed as possible, but you will be straightening your arm out so that there is no angle at the elbow. If you like, you can actually push back against something. In a chair, for example, you can let your arm dangle over the side and push backward against one of the rear chair legs. On a bed you can just push straight down and feel tension in the muscle in the back part of your upper arm. Find a position where you can produce tension in your right triceps. Flex that muscle . . . concentrate on the tension . . . push as hard as you can . . . push it . . . and RELAX. *Let your arm relax as much as you can. Focus on that warm, relaxed sensation in the upper arm muscles and let that relaxed sensation spread throughout the arm.*

Now let's move over to the left arm. Again find something that you can push against so that you can produce tension in that left triceps muscle. Flex the muscle . . . concentrate on the tension . . . push . . . and RELAX. *Let the arm resume a comfortable position. Relax as much as possible. Focus your attention on that warm, relaxed feeling.*

Take a very deep breath. Hold it for one second and as you exhale very slowly, relax as much as you can. Take a deep breath . . . as you exhale RELAX . . . RELAX. *Let all the muscles become as relaxed as you can. You want to smooth them out.*

We are next going to relax some of the other muscle groups. As we do, you should try to keep your forearms, hands, and upper arm muscles as relaxed as possible. Try not to tense them any more. First of all, let's exercise some of the muscles in the shoulders and upper back. Shrug your shoulders in a very exaggerated fashion. Bring both of your shoulders up toward your ears . . . hold them as high as you can . . . higher . . . hold them . . . and RELAX. *Let your shoulders resume a comfortable position. Now concentrate on that warm, relaxed feeling in the shoulder muscles and along the upper part of your back. A very soothing sensation. You should make a mental note of what it feels like to have those muscles relaxed so that in the future you can turn on this relaxed feeling without having to tense them.* Concentrate on that warm, relaxed feeling.

Next we are going to work on some of the muscles in the neck. Start turning your head very slowly to the right. Turn it very slowly until you reach a point at which you can't turn it any more. When you get to that point, gently push a little bit further. You will feel tension along the left side of your neck. Push a little more . . . feel that tension . . . push . . . and RELAX. *Let the neck muscles smooth out. Allow your head to resume a comfortable position and concentrate on that very warm and pleasant sensation in the neck muscles.*

We will now exercise the opposing muscle groups. This time turn your head very slowly to the left. Very slowly, until you reach that sticking point. When you reach that point, push a little bit further until you feel tension along the right side of your neck. Push until you feel that tension . . . hold it there . . . hold it . . . and RELAX. *Let the muscles smooth out. Let your eyes resume a comfortable position and simply focus on the sensations that you now feel around the eye muscles.*

Using the opposing muscle group, close your eyes as tightly as you possibly can. Bring the eyeballs down and your cheek muscles up as tight as you can. You may even see stars. Tighten them as much as you can . . . concentrate on that tension . . hold it there . . . and RELAX. *Let the muscles go and focus on that warm, pleasant sensation you feel when you relax the muscles around the eyes.* You may find it comfortable simply to let your eyelids close. This allows you to pay more attention to these pleasant sensations.

One final muscle group that we will be working on in the facial area involves the muscles in your forehead. These muscles are again very important in what most people consider tension or muscular anxiety. You will frequently find after you practice these exercises that the forehead muscles are often those which tense first in anxiety situations. Pay particular attention to what it feels like to relax these muscles so that you will then be cued in everyday situations when you start becoming tense. In order to flex these muscles, wrinkle your forehead as much as you can and pull your nose muscles up toward your eyes. You should be pulling the forehead muscles down to form an exaggerated scowl. There are quite a few muscle groups involved here. Concentrate on tensing as many of them as you can . . . hold it there . . . hold it . . . and RELAX. *Concentrate on the warm, relaxed sensation.*

Take a few moments right now to inventory the muscles around your face. If any of them feel tense, try to relax away the tension without again flexing the muscles. Concentrate on the muscles of the forehead, around the eyes, and the jaw muscles. If you feel any tension whatsoever, try to relax it away so that all the muscles feel very smooth . . . very placid . . . and very relaxed.

Let's take a moment here to inventory the progress we have made. *Focus on the sensations in your shoulders. If you feel any tension there, relax it away. Now slowly guide your concentration down into the arms. They should be very comfortable. The upper arms should be very relaxed, both the front and back. Your forearms and the fingers should feel very limp and heavy. All of the muscles should be smoothed out and relaxed.* If you feel any tension whatsoever in these muscles, take a few seconds now to relax it slowly away. Continue the exercises below only when you have reached a calm, passive relaxation in your arms, shoulders, neck, and facial muscles.

Take a deep breath, hold it for one second, and *as you exhale very slowly, concentrate on becoming more and more relaxed. Let all the muscles smooth out and eliminate every bit of tension from your body.*

The next muscle group we will work with involves the abdominal muscles and some of the muscles in the chest and trunk region. As you exercise these areas, try to keep the rest of your body as relaxed as possible. Remember, your shoulders, neck, arms, and facial muscles should remain as relaxed as possible from here on out. Now then, tense the muscles in the stomach area by pushing them out. You are trying to make a ball with your stomach. Push the muscles out and around your stomach as much as you can. Concentrate on the tension as you push the muscles out . . . hold it there . . . and RELAX. *Let the muscles relax and concentrate on that warm sensation as they smooth out. You want to focus on what it feels like to relax those muscles and again allow that warm, pleasant sensation to spread to other areas in your body so that all of your muscles are as relaxed as possible.*

This time pull your stomach muscles in as much as possible. Pull them in so you are trying to touch your abdomen to your backbone. Pull them in as much as possible . . . feel that tension in the muscles . . . hold it there . . . and RELAX. *Let the muscles smooth out. Let that soothing, relaxed feeling overtake all of the muscles in the abdominal area, and allow yourself to sink deeper and deeper into this warm pool of relaxation. The muscles should feel very heavy, very limp—as if they were just hanging there.* You are doing nothing to support them. They are as relaxed as they can possibly be.

We are now going to move on to the muscles in your legs. As we work on these exercises, remember to keep your upper body, your arms, and your facial muscles as relaxed as you possibly can. We shall begin with the muscles in the upper part of your right leg. In order to exercise those muscles, stretch out your right leg so that you have straightened it and you have locked your knee. When you lock the knee push a little further you you will feel tension in the upper part of your right leg, particularly in the top part of the muscle. Stretch it so that you feel that tension. Tense it as much as possible. Hold it there . . . concentrate on the tension in the leg . . . and RELAX. *Let your leg resume a comfortable position and focus your attention on what it feels like to relax those large muscles in the upper leg.*

This time let's work on the muscle in the upper part of your left leg. Again straighten the leg out until you have locked the knee. Once you have locked the knee, tense the muscle in the upper part of the leg as much as you can. Concentrate on tensing that muscle . . . hold it there . . . hold it . . . and RELAX. *Let the muscles smooth out and concentrate on that warm, pleasant sensation. Allow that sensation to spread throughout the upper leg area so that you feel no tension whatsoever.*

Moving back to the right leg, we are now going to exercise the muscles in the calf area. Remember we are working only on the right leg now. Begin to push your toes away from you as if you were pushing down on a gas pedal. Push the toes away from you as far as you can. The muscles in your toes, in the ball of your foot, and in the calf area should feel very tense. Concentrate on pushing as much as you can. Tense those muscles . . . hold it there . . . and RELAX. *Let the muscles smooth out. Concentrate on what it feels like to relax those muscles.*

Now let's do it with the left leg. With the left leg only, push the toes away from you as far as you can until you feel tension in the ball of your left foot and in your left calf. Push as hard as you can . . . push even further . . . push . . . and RELAX. *Let the muscles smooth out and concentrate on allowing yourself to relax deeper and deeper so you feel no tension whatsoever in your legs. They feel very heavy and limp.*

Now let's try it with both feet at the same time. Push with both feet. Push the toes away from you and pull the heels up toward you. Feel that tension in the calf muscles and the balls of your feet. Hold it there . . . concentrate on the tension . . . and RELAX. *Let them smooth out. Let the muscles relax as much as possible and focus your attention on those sensations.*

We are now going to exercise an opposing muscle group. Again let's use both legs at one time. However, instead of pushing the toes away from you, this time you should pull them toward you. Pull your toes upward, and the heels should be going away from you. It is as if you are trying to lift a weight with your toes alone. You should be pulling your toes toward your knees. Concentrate on producing as much tension as you can in the calf area and in the lower part of your ankles. Feel tension in both feet. Pull the toes toward you . . . concentrate on that tension . . . hold it there . . . and RELAX. *Let the feet resume a comfortable position and concentrate on those warm, pleasant sensations as all of the muscles in the calf, ankle, and foot areas relax, smooth out, and assume a very warm, heavy, limp state.*

Take a deep breath, hold it for one second, and *as you exhale very slowly, concentrate on becoming more and more relaxed.* Try to let yourself smooth all of the muscles out. You should feel no tension whatsoever.

Take a very slow inventory starting with your feet and moving up your body from one section to the next. If you feel any tension whatsoever, try to relax it away without tensing the muscles. *Just allow that warm, pleasant, relaxed feeling to spread from one section to the next so that all of the muscles are very smooth . . . very relaxed. You should now have no tension in the feet . . . in the calves . . . in the upper legs . . . the abdomen area . . . chest . . . shoulders . . . neck . . . jaws . . . muscles around the eyes . . . the forehead . . . your upper arms . . . forearms . . . and hands. All of the muscles are very relaxed . . . they have smoothed out . . . and you feel no tension. Take a few seconds here to allow yourself to sink even deeper. If you are lying on a bed or sitting on a chair, allow yourself to sink even deeper. All of your weight should be supported by the couch, or bed, or chair. Your entire body should be limp and very relaxed.*

These exercises provide you with excellent training in what it feels like to be relaxed and what the cues are for muscular tension. As you practice the exercises, you should try to anticipate yourself somewhat so that you can learn to relax the muscles without even tensing them. Eventually you will be able to produce a very relaxed feeling in the major muscle groups within a matter of seconds. And even more important, you will start to pick up cues of muscular tension in everyday situations. These cues can be signals to you that you should take a few moments and relax yourself. You should also get into the habit of taking brief muscle inventories to find out whether you are muscularly tense in certain situations. Get in the habit of relaxing those muscles you do not need for a particular task. For example, you may notice that, as you drive, you often tense many muscles which are unnecessary for good driving skills. In that situation, try to relax all of those muscles which do not need to be tense—such as the facial or forehead muscles. Try to relax yourself as much as possible without turning off the muscles you need for the task at hand.

A helpful relaxation manual that includes a recording of similar instructions is provided by Douglas A. Bernstein and Thomas D. Borkovec in *Progressive Relaxation Training* (Research Press, 1973).

Self-Instructional Skills

What you say to yourself can have a dramatic effect on both your feelings and your behavior. The private monologues that run through your head most of the day are frequent culprits in your feelings of distress and dissatisfaction. It is therefore worthwhile to "tune in" to those private conversations and evaluate their impact on your happiness. This is not as easy as it sounds because most of us take our thoughts for granted and we are not experienced at observing them.

There are several ways to improve your self-talk so that it works *for* you rather than against you. As pointed out in chapter 8, the first step in these strategies is to identify the contents of your private conversations. Three of the most popular ways for "tuning in" on your own thoughts are as follows:

1. Try to vividly imagine yourself in one of your problem situations and—as you act out your mental movie—pay close attention to your fantasies and self-talk.
2. Carry a small card or notebook with you and, at the first sign of your unpleasant feelings, do an "instant replay" of the thoughts and images that preceded your distress.
3. Buy a small portable timer (e.g., a parking meter timer) and set it for different intervals throughout the day (from ten- to sixty-minute intervals). When the timer buzzes, write down everything you were thinking and feeling at that specific moment.
4. Keep a personal diary in which you write down your most intimate and candid beliefs about yourself and your problem.

Identifying your thoughts and fantasies is an important first step, but you will still face the task of altering these private events. Some of the most promising options for changing them were briefly mentioned in chapter 8. These included the following:

1. Evaluate your thoughts in terms of their logic. Are you exaggerating? Watch for such words as "always" and "never": they are

frequent signs that you are painting a black-and-white picture when it may not be appropriate. Also common is the tendency to focus on things that *support* your beliefs and attitudes and to ignore or discount those that challenge it. Be careful not to generalize to a global pronouncement on the basis of a few isolated instances.

2. Try to come up with alternative ways of thinking. This may seem difficult at first, and the comments of a supportive friend or spouse may be helpful. Write down your alternative thoughts and be prepared to plug them in as challenges when the old troublemaking thoughts occur.

3. Experiment with what it would feel like if you actually *believed* your new set of thoughts. In the beginning this may seem futile or inauthentic, but you can often get past this by remembering that you are just pretending for a while—that you are "trying on" a new set of beliefs and that you always have the option of not buying them.

4. Try to think of experiments you could perform to actually *test* some of your old assumptions. For example, if you believe that people wouldn't like you if you were really "yourself" in social situations, devise a personal experiment to test this.

5. Develop an open and honest relationship with someone you trust and share some of your thoughts with them. Their feedback may help you gain some perspective on points on which you are biased in your thinking and how you might go about changing your everyday self-talk.

A helpful guide to identifying and altering some of these thought patterns is offered in *A Guide to Rational Living* by Albert Ellis and Robert A. Harper (Wilshire, 1961).

Gradation Skills

One of the most powerful strategies for approaching a difficult challenge is to divide it into small, manageable steps and tackle them one at a time. Just as it is often more comfortable to ease yourself into a tub of very hot water, it appears that slow and gradual steps toward a personal problem may often facilitate its resolution. One simple way to accomplish this is to outline the task as if it were the staircase illustrated in figure 14.

The lowest step is your location right now, and the highest step is the ultimate goal you would like to achieve. (Take care to avoid a perfectionistic or unreasonable goal!) Next, fill in each step with a performance or task that is just slightly more challenging than the one before it. In the staircase shown in figure 14–1 there are ten steps, but you should feel free to divide your own efforts into much smaller units. Generally speaking, the smaller the steps, the more likely the progress. Don't make the mistake of trying to tackle too much too soon. If you find that the distance between two steps is greater than you had anticipated, simply compromise by inserting some smaller steps in between. Likewise, it is often helpful to combine your gradation strategy with relaxation training or improved self-talk. These latter skills will help you cope with some of the apprehension and discomfort that are inevitable in any challenging situation.

As you progress up your personal staircase, be sure to concentrate your attention on the immediate step you are working on —don't keep thinking about the distance between you and your ultimate goal. Progress is made one step at a time; failures are often made in leaps. To motivate your perseverance up the staircase, you may want to establish a personal incentive system and reward yourself for each step mastered. The cooperation and encouragement of friends and family is also a welcome element.

Mental Practice Skills

One of the more subtle and yet powerful strategies for achieving self-change is mental practice—the imaginary rehearsal of the performance or experience about which you are concerned. Mental practice skills can be improved by setting

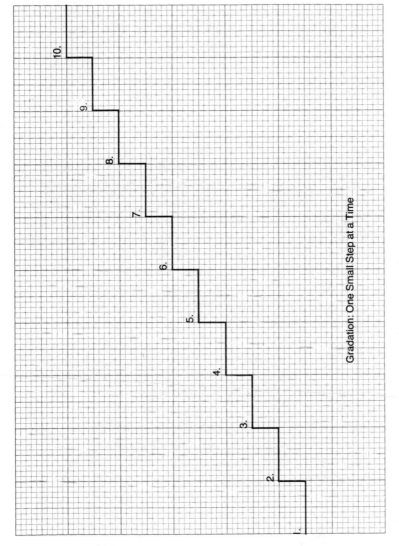

Gradation: One Small Step at a Time

Figure 14

aside time to concentrate on their development and refinement. Although some people experience initial difficulty in forming mental images, a little practice will often result in satisfactory results. Normally, your ability to produce vivid mental images is increased when you are relaxed and lying down. Distracting noises and lights should be reduced as much as possible.

Begin by simply concentrating on a familiar scene. For example, you can start by opening your eyes and studying the room you are in. Look for details—the location of furniture, the position of curtains, and the shape of shadows. Now slowly close your eyes and try to maintain that picture. If you begin to lose it, open your eyelids partway so that you can see the room only dimly. Try to fill in the rest of the details with your imagination. After practicing this for several minutes, you should be able to "see" the room mentally.

Next, concentrate on your other senses. With your eyes closed try to pay close attention to what you hear. Are there faint noises outside? Can you hear your own breathing? What about smells—can you identify any familiar smells? Finally, concentrate on your sense of touch. What does it feel like to be lying where you are? Can you feel where your body is touching the bed or couch? What are your hands touching? Can you sense the weight of your clothes? These may seem like strange questions, but they are often helpful in focusing attention on sensations that are often overlooked.

When you are ready to mentally practice your target performance, be sure to concentrate on making your mental movie as real as possible. Many people find it helpful to think of themselves as actually "climbing into" the mental movie they are creating. Start your movie earlier than the target performance. Begin, for example, with breakfast on the day of your performance. Try to "feel" yourself at the breakfast table and see if you can hear the sounds of morning traffic or can smell the food you are eating. As you move toward your performance in your mental movie, try to maintain this vividness and attention to details.

When you get to the part of your movie at which you are starting to approach your target performance, concentrate on being as realistic as possible. If you would be frightened or angry in real life, try to experience these feelings in your imagery. Execute your coping strategies to deal with these unpleasant sensations and allow your movie to play itself out to a satisfactory ending. Be careful not to make it look unrealistically easy, but at the same time you should not allow it to end as a tragedy. It is not uncommon for people to begin mental practice and then find that their movie turns into a horror show that portrays their worst fears. If this happens, roll back the mental film and play the scene over. Do imaginary "retakes" until you have performed your target behavior in a reasonably efficient manner. By practicing this skill prior to real-life challenges, you can not only correct some of your inaccurate expectations, but you can refine some of your skills for coping with the challenge that lies before you.

14

Getting in Gear

Thoughts are but dreams till their effects be tried.
—SHAKESPEARE

If you have not already begun to experiment with a PPS approach to your own personal problem, this chapter is designed to help you get started. If you are experiencing any serious reservations about the promise of undertaking a self-change project, you may want to look back at chapter 2 and to examine some of your own assumptions about the possibility of personal change. As mentioned in the early chapters of this book, no guarantees can in good conscience be offered in the field of human behavior change. We are still in the process of learning about some of the complex factors that influence our patterns of thought, feeling, and action. The horizon is hardly hopeless, however, and the strategies outlined in this book represent some of the most promising methods now employed by mental health specialists. While skepticism is a healthy attitude in many realms of daily experience, it may become harmful when it prevents you from exploring a potentially beneficial option in your life.

The PPS system is specifically devoted to personal effectiveness—to helping you identify problem solving strategies that work for you. There is nothing mysterious about the process, nor does it require an unusual amount of intelligence, motivation, or prerequisite skills. All that is required is a willingness to experiment with strategies that have already affected the lives and happiness of many other people. Let's turn our attention to the PPS sequence and how you might go about exploring its relevance for your own self-change goals. When you actually begin your own PPS analysis, it may be worthwhile to review each chapter as you enter a new stage of the sequence.

S: Specifying the General Problem

Recall that in the first stage of PPS your primary focus is on defining your problem. Since a personal problem always involves a felt discrepancy between the way things are and the way you would like them to be, your attention here should be concentrated on *how* you feel and in what sphere of your life. Table 5 is designed to help you specify your problem and to establish reasonable goals for self-improvement. Remember that it is usually better to work on one problem at a time and to start with your least difficult problem. This will allow you to concentrate all your energy in one area and to develop valuable PPS skills for your more challenging later problems. When you indicate your goals, be sure to think about their reasonableness and feasibility.

C: Collecting Information

In the second stage of PPS you begin your personal detective work by collecting important information about the circumstances surrounding your problem. Accurate personal information will not only help you identify possible causes of your problem: it may also suggest promising solutions. In addition, your personal records will play an important role in your later evaluation of the effects of a self-change strategy. The need for accuracy in your record keeping cannot be overemphasized.

Table 5
Specifying Your Problem

1. *Identification of Feelings*
   I feel _____

   _____

   _____

2. *Area of Felt Discrepancy*
   My feelings are associated with a dissatisfaction about _____

   _____

   _____

3. *Ranking of Problems* (when more than one is present)
   Out of the problems I now face, I believe that _____
   is my least difficult problem, followed in order of difficulty by

   _____

   My immediate focus in PPS will be on my problem in the area of

   _____

4. *Goal Setting*
   Over the next _____ weeks I would like to see some improvement
   in my problem. In the long-run, I think it is reasonable to work toward

   _____

Inaccurate information may lead you to ineffective solutions.
For suggestions about what information to collect, look back
at table 2 in chapter 6. The PPS diary form is shown again in
figure 15. You may want to make copies of this form so that
you can carry it around with you in everyday situations. Remember that it is important to record your target experiences
as soon as they occur—your memory can often be misleading.
A *minimum* of ten days of record keeping is necessary to get
an accurate picture (unless you are *sure* that your problem is
not influenced by a recurrent pattern). If your target experience occurs very infrequently, you may need to extend your
initial period of record keeping. Bear in mind that your target
may begin to change simply because you are paying attention
to it. If this occurs, extend your record keeping until the target

Figure 15
PPS Diary

Date _____ Target _____

Time	Place	Persons Present	Preceding Thoughts	Preceding Actions or Events	Subsequent Thoughts	Subsequent Actions or Events	Comments

reaches a satisfactory level or until it stops changing. When you are confident that you have an accurate picture of the way things are, you should not simply abandon your personal records. Instead, shift to the short form of the PPS diary (see figure 16). This will enable you to keep tabs on your progress and to later evaluate the impact of your self-change program.

I: Identifying Patterns

The causes of a personal problem are always current, and they tend to fall into one or more of the following categories: (1) the situation itself, (2) your behavior patterns, and (3) your thought patterns. If you have good reason to believe that your problem stems from a recent "one-shot" occurrence, you can move on to stage four. Otherwise you need to spend some time looking for recurrent patterns in your problem. This may be aided by looking back at figure 5 in chapter 7. Another possible aid in helping you identify patterns is shown in table 6. As you write your responses to the various questions posed there, it may be helpful to have your diary forms in front of you. Also, if you have difficulty detecting any consistent patterns in your problem, ask a close friend or family member to go over your records with you. This often introduces an element of objectivity and may offer an important addition to your own detective skills.

E: Examining Possible Solutions

Problem solutions are strategies that effectively reduce the felt discrepancy between the way things are and the way you would like them to be. This is most often accomplished by altering the circumstances that surround your problem, by changing relevant thought patterns, or by altering your behavior. More often than not, all three of these strategies may be combined.

Figure 16
PPS Diary (Short Form)

Dates _____

Target _____

	Sunday	Monday	Tuesday	Wednesday	Thursday	Friday	Saturday
Morning (midnight to noon)							
Afternoon (noon to 6 P.M.)							
Evening (6 P.M. to midnight)							
Daily Total							

Weekly Total: _____   _____ Daily Average: _____

Comments: _____

Table 6
Identifying Patterns

1. Does your problem occur more frequently or intensely at specific times of day? On particular days of the week?

2. What is your physical location when your problem usually occurs?

3. Are certain persons consistently present when you experience your problem?

4. What thoughts or fantasies immediately *precede* your problem experience?

5. What thoughts or fantasies accompany or follow your problem experience?

6. List the times and situations when your problem is least likely to occur.

7. If your personal records indicate any instances when you expected to experience your problem but did not, write down what may have made the difference in those instances.

As noted in chapter 8 and expanded in chapter 13, thought patterns may often be changed by a four-step sequence that involves

1. identifying thoughts and fantasies that may be contributing to your problem
2. evaluating the reasonableness of these thoughts
3. developing and practicing alternative beliefs about yourself and your problem
4. experimenting with these new patterns of thought by tentatively acting as if they were true

Whenever possible, you should try to put your old assumptions to the test by checking them against reality. Many people are surprised to find that they have lived much of their lives based on assumptions and beliefs that were simply unwarranted.

In changing your behavior patterns, there are at least six basic strategies to choose from. You can—

1. focus on developing relaxation or meditational skills;
2. develop and practice self-talk that will help you handle your problem more satisfactorily;
3. practice your target performance mentally;
4. divide your challenge into small steps of gradually increasing difficulty and tackle one at a time;
5. choose someone as a model whom you can imitate in dealing with your problem;
6. establish incentives for persisting in your self-change efforts or making gradual progress toward your goal.

There are certain "do's and dont's" for each of these strategies, so it may be well worth your while to review the material in chapters 8 and 13.

If you decide that your self-change project might benefit from the inclusion of strategies that focus on the alteration of your everyday environment, four basic methods were discussed:

1. the arrangement of special cues or prompts to help interrupt old habitual patterns and instigate more desirable ones
2. the intentional avoidance of situations that are most difficult for you
3. the rearrangement of your everyday environment so that it no longer encourages your problem
4. the enlistment of cooperation and support from friends, family members, and co-workers

The importance of this last element is difficult to exaggerate. Your chances for successful self-change are much greater when your efforts take place in the context of a supportive social environment.

N: Narrowing and Trying

Before you launch a self-change project, it is important that you give careful thought to the options that are available. It is often helpful to write down as many strategies as possible that might produce improvement. You can then narrow these options by eliminating those that seem unfeasible or least likely to succeed. Table 7 offers a useful checklist for evaluating your self-change strategy before you actually begin it.

Be sure to watch out for unreasonable standards and all-or-none thinking in the options you have selected. Also, the mental movie "test run" is a critically informative exercise—don't forget it. Finally, to help get yourself started, why not make up a formal self-change contract like the one illustrated in table 3 of chapter 9? This contract will aid you in specifying what you plan to do, when you will start, and how long you will continue your first personal experiment. The contract also asks

Table 7
Option Checklist

1. Does my proposed solution actually focus on changing some of the patterns I have identified?

2. Is my solution too ambitious? Am I asking for too much too soon? Will I *really* be able to implement it?

3. Have I overlooked any obstacles that might stand in the way of my solution?

4. Is the solution worse than the problem?

5. Am I allowing enough time for my solution to take effect?

6. How might I improve my proposed solution?

7. Have I performed a mental "test run" to check out the promise of my strategy?

your witnesses to be cooperative and encouraging. Don't assume that this brief statement on the contract will be enough to enlist their support, however. If you really want them to work "with" you rather than "against" you, have a sincere talk with them in which you emphasize the importance of their support. During your project, be sure to express your appreciation when they are helpful.

C: Comparing Your Progress

Keep in mind that your immediate goal is improvement, not a miraculous overnight resolution. Your accurate personal records will be important in helping you gauge your progress. Also helpful may be a chart on which you plot your self-change. Figure 17 offers a blank chart, but you can construct one of your own on simple graph paper. Let the horizontal axis represent time (usually days or weeks) and the vertical axis represent the frequency, duration, or intensity of your target experience. If your target is one that fluctuates widely from one day to the next, it may be helpful to average your records over weekly intervals. Likewise, if your problem occurs very infrequently, you may have to allow longer time intervals to assess the impact of your self-change strategy.

As you look for progress, keep in mind that you are looking for any change in the frequency, duration, intensity, or patterning of your target experience. If that change is disappointingly small, remember that the resolution to a problem is simply the accumulation of small improvements.

E: Evaluation

Be careful not to cast your personal experiment in terms of all-or-none success or failure. Few problem solvers (including the professional experts) obtain the results they want with their very first solution. Keep in mind that perseverance pays off and

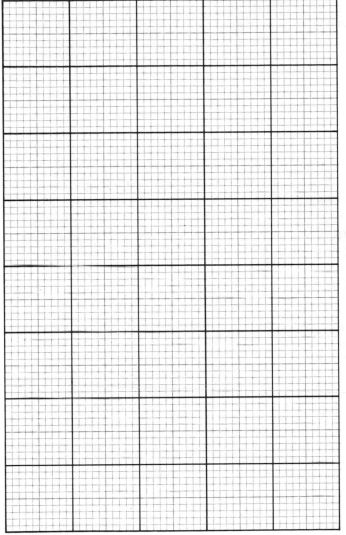

Personal Progress Chart

Figure 17

that a personal experiment is only a failure if you do not learn something from it. If your initial results were entirely satisfactory, consider yourself fortunate (or extremely skillful at pps) and enjoy your progress. More often than not, however, your first strategy will produce some improvements, but it will leave ample room for others. In these cases—which are the most common—you should integrate your new insights into a revised strategy and undertake a refined self-change project. If you detected absolutely no progress during your project, ask yourself the questions listed in table 8. These will usually suggest a reason for such unsatisfactory results.

Whatever the results of your first experiment, it is important that you recognize that responsibility is shared by you and your environment. Within certain limits, you can take an active role in changing that environment so that it is more conducive to

Table 8
Evaluating a "No-Progress" Experiment

1. Are you confident that your personal records are accurate and complete?

2. Were you conscientious and consistent in carrying out your self-change strategy?

3. Did you allow sufficient time for the strategy to show an impact?

4. Were there any unusual circumstances that might have jeopardized your progress?

5. Are you confident that you have examined *all* possible signs of improvement (frequency, intensity, duration, and patterning)?

6. Are you confident that your definition of the problem was accurate?

7. What have you learned about the factors that may be contributing to your problem?

8. What kind of changes would be necessary to put together a more promising self-change strategy?

the life-style you would like to develop. Don't sell yourself short on skills and don't assume that your problem is insurmountable until you have really tested that assumption. If it does turn out that you must compromise some of your goals in order to reduce the felt discrepancy between the way things are and the way you would like them to be, this can be a reasonable and satisfying resolution. Compromising how you want things to be is only unfortunate when you have not first tested the limits of your ability to change them.

Finally, you should bear in mind that professional counseling is an ever present option in your PPS efforts. There is nothing wrong or dishonorable about seeking the advice and support of an expert. The experts themselves often rely on one another for feedback and assistance in their pursuits of personal growth, and you are wise to keep this in mind if your PPS efforts do not eventually produce the results you desire. Your ultimate commitment should be to your own personal development, and your options must be dictated by your needs. Remember that personal growth is a journey that will never be completed. To the extent that you remain committed to that growth, your future is destined to be full of rich and rewarding experiences.

Bibliography

Anthony, J., & Edelstein, B. A. Thought-stopping treatment of anxiety attacks due to seizure-related obsessive ruminations. *Journal of Behavior Therapy and Experimental Psychiatry*, 1975, *6*, 343–344.

Arnkoff, D. B., & Stewart, J. The effectiveness of modeling and videotape feedback on personal problem solving. *Behaviour Research and Therapy*, 1975, *13*, 127–133.

Ballard, K. D., & Glynn, T. Behavioral self management in story writing with elementary school children. *Journal of Applied Behavior Analysis*, 1975, *8*, 387–398.

Bandura, A. *Principles of behavior modification*. New York: Holt, Rinehart & Winston, 1969.

Bandura, A. Vicarious and self-reinforcement processes. In R. Glaser (Ed.), *The nature of reinforcement*. New York: Academic Press, 1971. Pp. 228–278.

Bandura, A. Behavior theory and the models of man. *American Psychologist*, 1974, *29*, 859–869.

Bandura, A., & Mahoney, M. J. Maintenance and transfer of self-reinforcement functions. *Behaviour Research and Therapy*, 1974, *12*, 89–98.

Bandura, A., Mahoney, M. J., & Dirks, S. J. Discriminative activation and maintenance of contingent self-reinforcement. *Behaviour Research and Therapy*, 1976, *14*, 1–6.

Bass, B. A. Reinforcement history as a determinant of self-reinforcement. *Journal of Psychology*, 1972, *81*, 195–203.

Bass, B. A. An unusual behavioral technique for treating obsessive ruminations. *Psychotherapy: Theory, Research and Practice*, 1973, *10*, 191–192.

Bayer, C. A. Self-monitoring and mild aversion treatment of trichotillomania. *Journal of Behavior Therapy and Experimental Psychiatry*, 1972, *3*, 139–141.

Beck. A. T. Thinking and depression. *Archives of General Psychiatry*, 1963, *9*, 324–333.

Beck, A. T. Cognitive therapy: Nature and relation to behavior therapy. *Behavior Therapy*, 1970, *1*, 184–200.

Beck. A. T. Role of fantasies in psychotherapy and psychopathology. *Journal of Nervous and Mental Disease*, 1970, *150*, 3–17.

Beck. A. T. Cognition, affect, and psychopathology. *Archives of General Psychiatry*, 1971, *24*, 495–500.

Beck, A. T. Cognition, anxiety, and psychophysiological disorders. In C. D. Spielberger (Ed.), *Anxiety: Current trends in theory and research.* New York: Academic Press, 1972. Pp. 343–354.

Beck, A. T. *Cognitive therapy and the emotional disorders.* New York: International Universities Press, 1976.

Bellack, A. S. A comparison of self-reinforcement and self-monitoring in a weight reduction program. *Behavior Therapy*, 1976, *7*, 68–75.

Bellack, A. S., Glanz, L. M., & Simon, R. Self-reinforcement style and covert imagery in the treatment of obesity. *Journal of Consulting and Clinical Psychology*, 1976, *44*, 490–491.

Bender, N. N. Self-verbalization versus tutor verbalization in modifying impulsivity. *Journal of Educational Psychology*, 1976, *68*, 347–354.

Beneke, W.M., & Harris, M. B. Teaching self-control of study behavior. *Behaviour Research and Therapy*, 1972, *10*, 35–41.

Berger, S., & Kanfer, F. H. Self-control: Effects of training and presentation delays of competing responses on tolerance of noxious stimulation. *Psychological Reports*, 1975, *37*, 1312–1314.

Bergin, A. E., & Garfield, S. L. (Eds.), *Handbook of psychotherapy and behavior change.* New York: Wiley, 1971.

Bernstein, D. A. Modification of smoking behavior: An evaluative review. *Psychological Bulletin*, 1969, *71*, 418–440.

Bernard, H. S., & Efran, J. S. Eliminating versus reducing smoking using pocket timers. *Behaviour Research and Therapy*, 1972, *10*, 399–401.

Best, J. A. Tailoring smoking withdrawal procedures to personality and motivational differences. *Journal of Consulting and Clinical Psychology*, 1975, *43*, 1–8.

Best, J. A., & Steffy, R. A. Smoking modification tailored to subject characteristics. *Behavior Therapy*, 1971, *2*, 177–191.

Bishop, B. R. Self-control is learned: External control precedes self-control. In J. S. Stumphauzer (Ed.), *Behavior therapy with delinquents.* Springfield, Ill.: Charles C. Thomas, 1973, Pp. 54–65.

Blackwood, R. The operant conditioning of verbally mediated self-control in the classroom. *Journal of School Psychology*, 1970, *8*, 257–258.

Blackwood, R. *Mediated self-control: An operant model of rational behav-*

ior. Akron, Ohio: Exordium Press, 1972.

Blechman, E. A. The family contract game: A tool to teach interpersonal problem solving. *Family Coordinator,* 1974, *23,* 269–281.

Blechman, E. A., Olson, D. H. L., Schornagel, C. Y., Halsdorf, M., & Turner, A. I. The family contract game: Technique and case study. *Journal of Consulting and Clinical Psychology,* 1976, *44,* 449–455.

Bolstad, O. D., & Johnson, S. M. Self-regulation in the modification of disruptive classroom behavior. *Journal of Applied Behavior Analysis,* 1972, *5,* 443–454.

Bornstein, P. H., & Quevillon, R. P. The effects of a self-instructional package on overactive preschool boys. *Journal of Applied Behavior Analysis,* 1976, *9,* 179–188.

Brightwell, D. R., & Clancy, J. Self-training of new eating behavior for weight reduction. *Diseases of the Nervous System,* 1976, *37,* 85–89.

Bristol, M. M., & Sloane, H. N. Effects of contingency contracting on study rate and test performance. *Journal of Applied Behavior Analysis,* 1974, *7,* 271–285.

Broden, M., Hall, R. V., & Mitts, B. The effect of self-recording on the classroom behavior of two eighth-grade students. *Journal of Applied Behavior Analysis,,* 1971, *4,* 191–199.

Burns, D. J., & Powers, R. B. Choice and self-control in children: A test of Rachlin's model. *Bulletin of the Psychonomic Society,* 1975, *5,* 156–158.

Cabush, D. & Edwards, K. Training clients to help themselves: Outcome effects of training college student clients in facilitative self-responding. *Journal of Counseling Psychology,* 1976, *23,* 34–39.

Caddy, G. R. & Lovibond, S. H. Self-regulation and discriminated aversive conditioning in the modification of alcoholics' drinking behavior. *Behavior Therapy,* 1976, *7,* 223–230.

Carkhuff, R. R. *The art of problem solving.* Amherst, Mass.: Human Resource Development Center, 1973.

Chang-Liang, R., & Denney, D. R. Applied relaxation as training in self-control. *Journal of Counseling Psychology,* 1976, *23,* 183–189.

Chaplin, S. M., & Karoly, P. Role of contract negotiation in self-management of study time: A preliminary investigation. *Psychological Reports,* 1975 *37,* 724–726.

Coche, E., & Flick, A. Problem-solving training groups for hospitalized psychiatric patients. *Journal of Psychology,* 1975, *91,* 19–29.

Corbin, C. B. Mental practice. In W. P. Morgan (Ed.), *Ergogenic aids and muscular performance.* New York: Academic Press, 1972, Pp. 93–118.

Craighead, W. E., Kazdin, A. E., & Mahoney, M. J. *Behavior modification: Principles, issues, and applications.* Boston: Houghton Mifflin, 1976.

Davis, G. A. *Psychology of human problem solving: Theory and practice.* New York: Basic Books, 1973.

Drabman, R. S., Spitalnik, R., & O'Leary, K. D. Teaching self-control to disruptive children. *Journal of Abnormal Psychology,* 1973, *82, 10–16.*

D'Zurilla, T. J., & Goldfried, M. R. Problem solving and behavior modification. *Journal of Abnormal Psychology*, 1971, *78*, 107–126.

Ellis, A. *Reason and emotion in psychotherapy.* New York: Stuart, 1962.

Emmelkamp, P. M. G. Self-observation versus flooding in the treatment of agoraphobia. *Behaviour Research and Therapy*, 1974, *12*, 229–237.

Emmelkamp, P. M. G., & Ultee, K. A. A comparison of "successive approximation" and "self-observation" in the treatment of agoraphobia. *Behavior Therapy*, 1974, *5*, 606–613.

Epstein, L. H., & Peterson, G. L. The control of undesired behavior by self-imposed contingencies. *Behavior Therapy*, 1973, *4*, 91–95.

Epstein, L. H., Webster, J. S., & Miller, P. M. Accuracy and controlling effects of self-monitoring as a function of concurrent responding and reinforcement. *Behavior Therapy*, 1975, *6*, 654–666.

Ernst, F. A. Self-recording and counterconditioning of a self-mutilative compulsion. *Behavior Therapy*, 1973, *4*, 144–146.

Evans, J. R., & Cody, J. J. Transfer of decision-making skills learned in a counseling-like setting to similar and dissimilar situations. *Journal of Counseling Psychology*, 1969, *16*, 427–432.

Felixbrod, J. J., & O'Leary, K. D. Effects of reinforcement on children's academic behavior as a function of self-determined and externally imposed contingencies. *Journal of Applied Behavior Analysis*, 1973, *6*, 241–250.

Ferster, C. B., Nurnberger, J. I., & Levitt, E. B. The control of eating. *Journal of Mathetics*, 1962, *1*, 87–109.

Flaxman, J. Quitting smoking. In W. E. Craighead, A. E. Kazdin, & M. J. Mahoney (Eds.), *Behavior modification: Principles, issues, and applications.* Boston: Houghton Mifflin, 1976. Pp. 414–430.

Frederiksen, L. W. Treatment of ruminative thinking by self-monitoring. *Journal of Behavior Therapy and Experimental Psychiatry*, 1975, *6*, 258–259.

Frederiksen, L. W., Epstein, L. H., & Kosevsky, B. P. Reliability and controlling effects of three procedures for self-monitoring smoking. *Psychological Record*, 1975, *25*, 255–264.

Frederiksen, L. W., & Fredriksen, C. B. Teacher-determined and self-determined token reinforcement in a special education classroom. *Behavior Therapy*, 1975, *6*, 310–314.

Glynn, E. L. Classroom applications of self-determined reinforcement. *Journal of Applied Behavior Analysis*, 1970, *3*, 123–132.

Glynn, E. L., & Thomas, J. D. Effect of cueing on self-control of classroom behavior. *Journal of Applied Behavior Analysis*, 1974, *7*, 299–306.

Glynn, E. L., Thomas, J. D., & Shee, S. M. Behavioral self-control of on-task behavior in an elementary classroom. *Journal of Applied Behavior Analysis*, 1973, *6*, 105–113.

Goldfried, M. R., Decenteceo, E., & Weinberg, L. Systematic rational restructuring as a self-control technique. *Behavior Therapy*, 1974, *5*, 247–254.

Goldfried, M. R., & Goldfried, A. P. Cognitive change methods. In F. H. Kanfer and A. P. Goldstein (Eds.) *Helping people change*. New York: Pergamon, 1975. Pp. 89–116.

Goldfried, M. R., & Merbaum, M. (Eds.), *Behavior change through self-control*. New York: Holt, Rinehart & Winston, 1973.

Goldfried, M. R., & Sobocinski, D. Effect of irrational beliefs on emotional arousal. *Journal of Consulting and Clinical Psychology*, 1975, *43*, 504–510.

Goldfried, M. R., & Trier, C. S. Effectiveness of relaxation as an active coping skill. *Journal of Abnormal Psychology*, 1974, *83*, 348–355.

Goldiamond, I. Self-control procedures in personal behavior problems. *Psychological Reports*, 1965, *17*, 851–868.

Goldstein, A. P., Heller, K., & Sechrest, L. P. *Psychotherapy and the psychology of behavior change*. New York: Wiley, 1966.

Goleman, D. J., & Schwartz, G. E. Meditation as an intervention in stress reactivity. *Journal of Consulting and Clinical Psychology*, 1976, *44*, 456–466.

Goodwin, S. & Mahoney, M. J. Modification of aggression via modeling: An experimental probe. *Journal of Behavior Therapy & Experimental Psychiatry*, 1975, *6*, 200–202.

Gottman, J. M., & McFall, R. M. Self-monitoring effects in a program for potential high school dropouts: A time-series analysis. *Journal of Consulting and Clinical Psychology*, 1972, *39*, 273–281.

Gulanick, N., Woodburn, L. T., & Rimm, D. C. Weight gain through self-control procedures. *Journal of Consulting and Clinical Psychology*, 1975, *43*, 536–539.

Haley, J. *Problem solving therapy*. San Francisco: Jossey-Bass, 1976.

Hauserman, N., Miller, J. S., & Bond, F. T. A behavioral approach to changing self-concept in elementary school children. *Psychological Record*, 1976, *26*, 111–116.

Hedberg, A. G., & Campbell, L. A comparison of four behavioral treatments of alcoholism. *Journal of Behavior Therapy and Experimental Psychiatry*, 1974, *5*, 251–256.

Hoon, P. W. Effects of self-monitoring and self-recording on ecological acts. *Psychological Reports*, 1976, *38*, 1285–1286.

Horan, J. J., Baker, S. B., Hoffman, A. M., & Shute, R. E. Weight loss through variations in the covarient control paradigm. *Journal of Consulting and Clinical Psychology*, 1975, *43*, 68–72.

Horan, J. J., Hoffman, A. M., & Macri, M. Self-control of chronic nailbiting. *Journal of Behavior Therapy and Experimental Psychiatry*, 1974, *5*, 307–309.

Hutzell, R. T., Platzek, D., & Logue, P. E. Control of symptoms of Gilles de la Tourette's syndrome by self-monitoring. *Journal of Behavior Therapy and Experimental Psychiatry*, 1974, *5*, 71–76.

Jason, L. Rapid improvement in insomnia following self-monitoring. *Journal*

of Behavior Therapy and Experimental Psychiatry, 1975, *6,* 349–350.
Johnson, S. M., & White, G. Self-observation as an agent of behavioral change. *Behavior Therapy,* 1971, *2,* 240–248.
Kanfer, F. H. Self-monitoring: Methodological limitations and clinical applications. *Journal of Consulting and Clinical Psychology,* 1970, *35,* 148–152.
Kanfer, F. H. Self-regulation: Research, issues and speculations. In C. Neuringer & J. L. Michael (Eds.), *Behavior modification in clinical psychology.* New York: Appleton-Century-Crofts, 1970. Pp. 178–220.
Kanfer, F., Karoly, P., & Newman, A. Reduction of children's fear of the dark by competence-related and situational threat-related verbal cues. *Journal of Consulting and Clinical Psychology,* 1975, *43,* 251–258.
Karoly, P., & Kanfer, F. H. Situational and historical determinants of self-reinforcement. *Behavior Therapy,* 1974, *5,* 381–390.
Kau, M. L., & Fischer, J. Self-modification of exercise behavior. *Journal of Behavior Therapy and Experimental Psychiatry,* 1974, *5,* 213–214.
Kazdin, A. E. Covert modeling and the reduction of avoidance behavior. *Journal of Abnormal Psychology,* 1973, *81,* 87–95.
Kazdin, A. E. The effect of model identity and fear-relevant similarity on covert modeling. *Behavior Therapy,* 1974, *5,* 624–635.
Kazdin, A. E. Effects of covert modeling and modeling reinforcement on assertive behavior. *Journal of Abnormal Psychology,* 1974, *83,* 240–252.
Kazdin, A. E. Comparative effects of some etfects of some variations of covert modeling. *Journal of Behavior Therapy and Experimental Psychiatry,* 1974, *5,* 225–231.
Kazdin, A. E. Covert modeling, model similarity, and reduction of avoidance behavior. *Behavior Therapy,* 1974, *5,* 325–340.
Kazdin, A. E. Reactive self-monitoring: The effects of response desirability, goal setting, and feedback. *Journal of Consulting and Clinical Psychology,* 1974, *42,* 704–716.
Kazdin, A. E. Self-monitoring and behavior change. In M. J. Mahoney & C. E. Thoresen (Eds.), *Self-control: Power to the person.* Monterey: Brooks/Cole, 1974. Pp. 218–246.
Kazdin, A. E. Effects of covert modeling, multiple models, and model reinforcement on assertive behavior. *Behavior Therapy,* 1976, *7,* 211–222.
Keller, J., Croake, J., & Brooking, J. Effects of a program in rational thinking on anxieties in older persons. *Journal of Counseling Psychology,* 1975, *22,* 54–57.
Kelly, A. H., & Curran, J. P. Comparison of a self-control approach and an emotional coping approach to the treatment of obesity. *Journal of Consulting and Clinical Psychology,* 1976, *44,* 683.
Kelly, G. A. *The psychology of personal constructs.* (2 vols.) New York: W. W. Norton, 1955.
Keutzer, C. S. Behavior modification of smoking: The experimental in-

vestigation of diverse techniques. *Behaviour Research and Therapy,* 1968, *6,* 137–157.

Kifer, R. E., Lewis, M. A., Green, D. R., & Phillips, E. L. Training predelinquent youths and their parents to negotiate conflict situations. *Journal of Applied Behavior Analysis,* 1974, *7,* 357–364.

Knapczyk, D. R., & Livingston, G. Self-recording and student teaching supervision: Variables within a token economy structure. *Journal of Applied Behavioral Analysis,* 1973, *6,* 481–486.

Kolb, D. A., & Boyatzis, R. E. Goal-setting and self-directed behavior change. *Human Relations,* 1970, *23,* 439–457.

Kopel, S., & Arkowitz, H. The role of attribution and self-perception in behavior change: Implications for behavior therapy. *Genetic Psychology Monographs,* 1975, *92,* 175–212.

Layne, C. C., Rickard, H. C., Jones, M. T., & Lyman, R. D. Accuracy of self-monitoring on a variable ratio schedule of observer verification. *Behavior Therapy,* 1976, *7,* 481–488.

Lazarus, A. A. *Behavior therapy and beyond.* New York: McGraw-Hill, 1971.

Lazarus, A. A. Multimodal behavior therapy: Treating the BASIC ID. *Journal of Nervous and Mental Disease,* 1973, *156,* 404–411.

Levendusky, P., & Pankrantz, L. Self-control techniques as an alternative to pain medication. *Journal of Abnormal Psychology,* 1975, *84,* 165–168.

Levinson, M., & Neuringer, C. Problem-solving behavior in suicidal adolescents. *Journal of Consulting and Clinical Psychology,* 1971, *37,* 433–436.

Lichtenstein, E. Modification of smoking behavior. *Journal of Consulting and Clinical Psychology,* 1971, *36,* 163–166.

Lichtenstein, E., Harris, D. E., Birchler, G. R., Wahl, J. M., & Schmahl, E. P. A comparison of rapid smoking, warm, smoky air, and attention-placebo in the modification of smoking behavior. *Journal of Consulting and Clinical Psychology,* 1973, *40,* 92–98.

Lichtenstein, E., & Keutzer, C. S. Experimental investigation of diverse techniques to modify smoking: A follow-up report. *Behaviour Research and Therapy,* 1969, *7,* 139–140.

Lipinski, D. P., Black, J. L., Nelson, R. O., & Ciminero, A. R. Influence of motivational variables on the reactivity and reliability of self-recording. *Journal of Consulting and Clinical Psychology,* 1975, *43,* 637–646.

Lipinski, D. P., & Nelson, R. O. The reactivity and unreliability of self-recording. *Journal of Consulting and Clinical Psychology,* 1974, *42,* 118–123.

Lira, F. T., Nay, W. R. McCullough, J. P., & Etkin, M. W. Relative effects of modeling and role playing in the treatment of avoidance behaviors. *Journal of Consulting and Clinical Psychology,* 1975, *43,* 608–618.

Lopatto, D., & Williams, J. L. Self-control: A critical review and an alternative interpretation. *The Psychological Record,* 1976, *26,* 3–12.

Mahoney, B. K., Rogers, T., Straw, M. K., & Mahoney, M. J. *Human obesity: Assessment and treatment.* Englewood Cliffs, N.J.: Prentice-Hall, 1979.

Mahoney, M. J. Research issues in self-management. *Behavior Therapy*, 1972, *3*, 45–63.

Mahoney, M. J. *Cognition and behavior modification.* Cambridge, Mass.: Ballinger, 1974.

Mahoney, M. J. Self-reward and self-monitoring techniques in weight control. *Behavior Therapy*, 1974, *5*, 48–57.

Mahoney, M. J. Personal science: A cognitive learning therapy. In A. Ellis and R. Grieger (Eds.), *Handbook of rational-emotive therapy.* New York: Springer, 1977.

Mahoney, M. J. (Ed.), *Cognition and clinical science.* New York: Plenum, 1979.

Mahoney, M. J., & Arnkoff, D. B. Cognitive and self-control therapies. In S. L. Garfield and A. E. Bergin (Eds.), *Handbook of psychotherapy and behavior change.* 2nd ed. New York: Wiley, 1978.

Mahoney, M. J., & Bandura, A. Self-reinforcement in pigeons. *Learning and Motivation*, 1972, *3*, 293–303.

Mahoney, M. J., Bandura, A., Dirks, S. J., & Wright, C. L. Relative preference for external and self-controlled reinforcement in monkeys. *Behaviour Research and Therapy*, 1974, *12*, 157–164.

Mahoney, M. J., & Mahoney, K. Treatment of obesity: A clinical exploration. In B. J. Williams, S. Martin, & J. P. Foreyt (Eds.), *Obesity: Behavioral approaches to dietary management.* New York: Bruner/Mazel, 1976. Pp. 30–39.

Mahoney, M. J., & Mahoney, K. *Permanent Weight Control.* New York: W. W. Norton, 1976.

Mahoney, M. J., & Thoresen, C. E. (Eds.), *Self-control: Power to the person.* Monterey, Calif.: Brooks/Cole, 1974.

Maletzky, B. M. Behavior recording as treatment: A brief note. *Behavior Therapy*, 1974, *5*, 107–111.

Masters, J. C., & Mokros, J. R. Self-reinforcement processes in children. In H. Reese (Ed.), *Advances in child development and behavior* (Vol. 9). New York: Academic Press, 1974.

Masters, J. C., & Santrock, J. W. Studies in the self-regulation of behavior: Effects of contingent cognitive and affective events. *Developmental Psychology*, 1976, *12*, 334–348.

McGuire, M. T., & Sifneos, P. E. Problem-solving in psychotherapy. *Psychiatric Quarterly*, 1970, *44*, 667–673.

McKenzie, T. L., & Rushall, B. S. Effects of self-recording on attendance and performance in a competitive swimming training environment. *Journal of Applied Behavior Analysis*, 1974, *7*, 199–206.

McReynolds, W. T., & Church, A. Self-control, study skills development, and counseling approaches to the improvement of study behavior. *Behaviour Research and Therapy*, 1973, *11*, 233–235.

Meichenbaum, D. The effects of instructions and reinforcement on thinking and language behaviors of schizophrenics. *Behaviour Research and Therapy*, 1969, *7*, 101–114.

Meichenbaum, D. Enhancing creativity by modifying what Ss say to themselves. *American Educational Research Journal*, 1975, *12*, 129–145.

Meichenbaum, D. A self-instructional approach to stress management: A proposal for stress inoculation training. In I. Sarason and C. D. Spielberger (Eds.), *Stress and anxiety* (Vol. 2). New York: Wiley, 1975. Pp. 227–263.

Meichenbaum, D. *Cognitive-behavior modification.* New York: Plenum, 1977.

Meichenbaum, D., Turk, D., & Burstein, S. The nature of coping with stress. In I. Sarason and C. D. Spielberger (Eds.), *Stress and anxiety* (Vol. 2). New York: Wiley, 1975. Pp. 337–360.

Mendonca, J. D., & Siess, T. F. Counseling for indecisiveness: Problem-solving and anxiety-management training. *Journal of Counseling Psychology*, 1976, *23*, 339–347.

Meyers, A., Mercatoris, M., & Artz, L. On the development of a cognitive self-monitoring skill. *Behavior Therapy*, 1976, *7*, 128–129.

Meyers, A., Mercatoris, M., & Sirota, A. Use of covert self-instruction for the elimination of psychotic speech. *Journal of Consulting and Clinical Psychology*, 1976, *44*, 480–482.

Mikulas, W. L. A televised self-control clinic. *Behavior Therapy*, 1976, *7*, 564–566.

Mischel W. Toward a cognitive social learning reconceptualization of personality. *Psychological Review*, 1973, *80*, 252–283.

Moleski, R., & Tosi, D. J. Comparative psychotherapy: Rational-emotive therapy versus systematic desensitization in the treatment of stuttering. *Journal of Consulting and Clinical Psychology*, 1976, *44*, 309–311.

Nelson, L. R., & Furst, M. L. An objective study of the effects of expectation on competitive performance. *Journal of psychology*, 1972, *81*, 69–72.

Nelson, R. O. Self-monitoring: Procedures and methodological issues. *Behavioral assessment: New directions in clinical psychology.* New York: Brunner/Mazel, 1976.

Nelson, R. O., Lipinski, D. P., & Black, J. L. The relative reactivity of external observations and self-monitoring. *Behavior Therapy*, 1976, *7*, 314–321.

Novaco, R. W. *Anger control: The development and evaluation of an experimental treatment.* Lexington, Mass.: D. C. Heath, 1975.

Novaco, R. W. Treatment of chronic anger through cognitive and relaxation controls. *Journal of Consulting and Clinical Psychology*, 1976, *44*, 681.

Ober, D. C. Modification of smoking behavior. *Journal of Consulting and Clinical Psychology*, 1968, *32*, 543–549.

Patterson, C. & Mischel, W. Effects of temptation-inhibiting and task facilitating plans on self-control. *Journal of Personality and Social Psychology*, 1976, *33*, 209–217.

Raimy, V. *Misunderstandings of the self.* San Francisco: Jossey-Bass, 1975.

Reeves, J. L. EMG-biofeedback reduction of tension headache: A cognitive skills-training approach. *Biofeedback and Self-Regulation*, 1976, *1*, 217–225.

Rehm, L. P., & Marston, A. R. Reduction of social anxiety through modification of self-reinforcement: An instigation therapy technique. *Journal of Consulting and Clinical Psychology,* 1968, *32,* 565–574.

Reschly, D. J. Consistency of self-reinforcement rates over different tasks, and sex, task success, and ability as determinants of rates of self-reinforcement. *Psychological Record,* 1973, *23,* 237–242.

Richards, C. S. Behavior modification of studying through study skills advice and self-control procedures. *Journal of Counseling Psychology,* 1975, *22,* 431–436.

Richards, C. S. Improving study behaviors through self-control techniques. In J. D. Krumboltz and C. E. Thoresen (Eds.), *Counseling methods.* New York: Holt, Rinehart & Winston, 1976. Pp. 462–467.

Richards, C. S., McReynolds, W. T., Holt, S., & Sexton, T. The effects of information feedback and self-administered consequences on self-monitoring study behavior. *Journal of Counseling Psychology,* 1976, *23,* 316–321.

Richards, C. S., Perri, M. G., & Gortney, C. Increasing the maintenance of self-control treatments through faded counselor contact and high information feedback. *Journal of Counseling Psychology,* 1976, *23,* 405–406.

Romanczyk, R. G. Self-monitoring in the treatment of obesity: Parameters of reactivity. *Behavior Therapy,* 1974, *5,* 531–540.

Rozensky, R. H. The effect of timing of self-monitoring behavior on reducing cigarette consumption. *Journal of Behavior Therapy and Experimental Psychiatry,* 1974, *5,* 301–303.

Rozensky, R. H., & Bellack, A. S. Behavior change and individual differences in self-control. *Behaviour Research and Therapy,* 1974, *12,* 267–268.

Rush, A. J., Beck, A. T. Kovacs, M., & Hollon, S. Comparative efficacy of cognitive therapy and pharmacotherapy in the treatment of depressed outpatients. *Cognitive Therapy and Research,* 1977, *1,* 17–38.

Rush, A. J., Khatami, M., & Beck, A. T. Cognitive and behavior therapy in chronic depression. *Behavior Therapy,* 1975, *6,* 398–404.

Sanchez-Craig, M. A self-control strategy for drinking tendencies. *Ontario Psychologist,* 1975, *7,* (4), 25–29.

Sanchez-Craig, M. Cognitive and behavioral coping strategies in the reappraisal of stressful social situations. *Journal of Counseling Psychology,* 1976, *23,* 7–12.

Sanchez-Craig, M. & Walker, K. Teaching alcoholics how to think defensively: A cognitive approach for the treatment of alcohol abuse. *Addictions,* 1975, *22* (3).

Santogrossi, D. A., O'Leary, K. D., Romanczyk, R. G., & Kaufman, K. F. Self-evaluation by adolescents in a psychiatric school token program. *Journal of Applied Behavior Analysis,* 1973, *6,* 277–287.

Sarason, I. G. Verbal learning, modeling, and juvenile delinquency. *American Psychologist,* 1968, *23,* 254–266.

Sarason, I. G. Test anxiety and the self-disclosing coping model. *Journal of Consulting and Clinical Psychology,* 1975, *43,* 148–153.

Sarason, I. G., & Ganzer, V. J. Modeling and group discussion in the rehabilitation of juvenile delinquents. *Journal of Counseling Psychology*, 1973, *20*, 442–449.

Schallow, J. R. Locus of control and success at self-modification. *Behavior Therapy*, 1975, *6*, 667–671.

Schmahl, D. P., Lichtenstein, E., & Harris, D. E. Successful treatment of habitual smokers with warm, smoky air and rapid smoking. *Journal of Consulting and Clinical Psychology*, 1972, *38*, 105–111.

Seligman, M. E. P. *Helplessness*. San Francisco: W. H. Freeman, 1975.

Seymour, F. W., & Stokes, T. F. Self-recording in training girls to increase work and evoke staff praise in an institution for offenders. *Journal of Applied Behavior Analysis*, 1976, *9*, 41–54.

Shapiro, D. H., & Zifferblatt, S. M. Zen meditation and behavioral self-control. *American Psychologist*, 1976, *31*, 519–532.

Shelton, J. L., & Ackerman, J. M. *Homework in counseling and psychotherapy*. Springfield, Ill.: Charles C. Thomas, 1974.

Sherman, A. R., & Plummer, I. L. Training in relaxation as a behavioral self-management skill: An exploratory investigation. *Behavior Therapy*, 1973, *4*, 543–550.

Shure, M. B., & Spivack, G. *A mental health program for kindergarten children*. Philadelphia: Hahnemann Medical College, 1974.

Shure, M. B., & Spivack, G. *Problem solving techniques in child rearing*. Philadelphia: Hahnemann Medical College, 1975.

Siegel, J. M., & Spivack, G. A new therapy program for chronic patients. *Behavior Therapy*, 1976, *7*, 129–130.

Siegel, J. M., & Spivack, G. Problem-solving therapy: The description of a new program for chronic psychiatric patients *Psychotherapy: Theory, Research and Practice*, 1976, *13*, 368–373.

Singer, J. L. *Imagery and daydream methods in psychotherapy and behavior modification*. New York: Academic Press, 1974.

Sipprelle, C. N. Induced anxiety. *Psychotherapy: Theory, Research and Practice*, 1967, *4*, 36–40.

Sobell, L. C., & Sobell, M. B. A self-feedback technique to monitor drinking behavior in alcoholics. *Behaviour Research and Therapy*, 1973, *11*, 237–238.

Spanos, N., Horton, C., & Chaves, J. The effect of two cognitive strategies on pain threshold. *Journal of Abnormal Psychology*, 1975, *84*, 677–682.

Speidel, G. E. Motivating effect of contingent self-reward. *Journal of Experimental Psychology*, 1974, *102*, 528–530.

Spiegler, M. D., Cooley, E. J., Marshall, G. J., Prince, H. T., & Puckett, S. P. A self-control versus a counterconditioning paradigm for systematic desensitization: An experimental comparison. *Journal of Counseling Psychology*, 1976, *23*, 83–86.

Spivack, G., Platt, J. J., & Shure, M. D. *The problem-solving approach to adjustment*. San Francisco: Jossey-Bass, 1976.

Spivack, G., & Shure, M. B. *Social adjustment of young children.* San Francisco: Jossey-Bass, 1974.

Stone, G. L., Hinds, W. C., & Schmidt, G. Teaching mental health behaviors to elementary school children. *Professional Psychology,* 1975, *6,* 34–40.

Stuart, R. B. Behavioral control of overeating. *Behaviour Research and Therapy,* 1967, *5,* 357–365.

Stuart, R. B. (Ed.), *Behavioral self-management: Strategies, techniques, and outcome.* New York: Brunner/Mazel, 1977.

Taylor, F. G., & Marshall, W. L. Experimental analysis of a cognitive-behavioral therapy for depression. *Cognitive Therapy and Research,* 1977, *1,* 59–72.

Tharp, R. G., Watson, D., & Kaya, J. Self-modification of depression. *Journal of Consulting and Clinical Psychology,* 1974, *42,* 624.

Thase, M. E., & Moss, M. K. The relative efficacy of covert modeling procedures and guided participant modeling on the reduction of avoidance behavior. *Journal of Behavior Therapy and Experimental Psychiatry,* 1976, *7,* 7–12.

Thomas, J. D. Accuracy of self-assessment of on-task behavior by elementary school children. *Journal of Applied Behavior Analysis,* 1976, *9,* 209–210.

Thoresen, C. E., & Mahoney, M. J. *Behavioral self-control.* New York: Holt, Rinehart & Winston, 1974.

Thorpe, G. L. Desensitization, behavior rehearsal, self-instructional training and placebo effects on assertive-refusal behavior. *European Journal of Behavioural Analysis and Modification,* 1975, *1,* 30–44.

Thorpe, G. L., Amatu, H. I., Blakey, R. S., & Burns, L. E. Contributions of overt instructional rehearsal and "specific insight" to the effectiveness of self-instructional training: A preliminary study. *Behavior Therapy,* 1976, *7,* 504–511.

Turkewitz, H., O'Leary, K. D., & Ironsmith, M. Generalization and maintenance of appropriate behavior through self-control. *Journal of Consulting and Clinical Psychology,* 1975, *43,* 577–583.

Vargas, J. M., & Adesso, V. J. A comparison of aversion therapies for nailbiting behavior. *Behavior Therapy,* 1976, *7,* 322–329.

Vincent, J. P., Weiss, R. L., & Birchler, G. R. A behavioral analysis of problem solving in distressed and nondistressed married and stranger dyads. *Behavior Therapy,* 1975, *6,* 475–487.

Watzlawick, P., Weakland, J., & Fisch, R. *Change: Principles of problem formation and problem resolution.* New York: W. W. Norton, 1974.

Wein, K. S., Nelson, R. O., & Odom, J. V. The relative contributions of reattribution and verbal extinction to the effectiveness of cognitive restructuring. *Behavior Therapy,* 1975, *6,* 459–474.

Weissberg, M. Anxiety-inhibiting statements and relaxation combined in two cases of speech anxiety. *Journal of Behavior Therapy and Experimental Psychiatry,* 1975, *6,* 163–164.

Williams, J. E. Self-monitoring of paranoid behavior. *Behavior Therapy,*
1976, *7,* 562.
Zastrow, C., & Chang, D. H. (Eds.), *The personal problem solver.* Englewood Cliffs, N.J.: Prentice-Hall, 1977.
Zimmerman, J. If it's what's inside that counts, why not count it? I:Self-
recording of feelings and treatment by "self-implosion." *Psychological
Record,* 1975, *25,* 3–16.